# LOOK INTO MY EYES

## *Asperger's, Hypnosis and Me*

Connect With Dan Jones: www.ALT-Solutions.org

**First Edition 2016**

**Published By Dan Jones**

**Copyright © Daniel Jones 2016**

Daniel Jones asserts the moral right to be identified as the author of this work

**ISBN 978-1530023905**

**Twitter: @AuthorDanJones #lookintomyeyes**

# CONTENTS

# CHAPTER ONE

## *Introduction*

This book isn't exactly a biography, detailing the story of my life; it is more like a biography through the lens of Asperger's, focusing on those areas of my life where Asperger's has played a role. My aim is to be open and honest about both the positive and negative aspects of myself. This book is for those interested in an Aspie-eyed perspective of the world, both internally and externally. This book is written by me, with my thinking style. I want the reader to see how my brain jumps around and makes associations - how I describe things and think about things from within my world, rather than dressing things up and trying to be something I'm not.

This could irritate some people. For example, one of my traits - which I have tried to minimise for the sake of the reader - is repetition. I don't notice I am doing it. I can find myself repeating the same things over and over without any awareness. Even writing a book and then reading what I have written, others can see my repetition, but I can review my work and not see repetition others say is there. I think that this is, in part, because I see things more literally than most; I can read two sentences someone else says are examples of repetition, and to me, they are two completely different sentences in two completely different contexts meaning two completely different things.

I try to give a taste of what it has been like to be me through different stages of my life, from birth to where I'm at currently. I have tried to be thorough in covering as much as possible and showing my learning and progress over the years. I want to make sure people can see how Asperger's impacts on all areas of life.

Having Asperger's can be overwhelming. Every moment can be a sensory overload. I can be walking through a town centre, and I will hear the jarring sounds of machines, and roaring motors of cars, and the chaos of hundreds of different people's voices, and movement coming from everywhere; I find myself constantly having to dodge people, having to try to adapt to people stopping and starting, darting my attention from face to face, and to dogs people are walking, and to movement of signs, and flashes of sunlight off windows, and to objects people are carrying. Normally, my only escape is to go into my mind and shut out as much as possible. I have tried to convey this chaos and sensory assault through my writing.

My main interest is hypnosis, which has featured heavily in my life, as it does in this book. Over a decade ago, I developed a few approaches to help get children to sleep through the way you read bedtime stories to children, and the way you interact with the child at bedtime. I shared and expanded upon these techniques in my 2006 and 2015 books, *Parenting Techniques That Work* and *Sleepy Bedtime Tales*. Hypnosis has taught me an immense amount about communication skills and how to begin to understand others. I have been fortunate enough to have the opportunity to teach hypnosis to others in workshops and through online courses and books. I also wrote a novel called *The Hypnotic Assassin* which is very blunt and to the point; I think the writing style reveals that it is written by someone with Asperger's. The novel was intended to be a creative way of teaching people about hypnosis through the use of a story.

**Structure of this book**

When I started thinking about how best to write this book, I thought about having someone help me to structure the book; but then, as I was writing what I wanted to include, I decided that I would like the book to be written as closely as possible to how my mind thinks about things. I was aware my mind jumps around from one thing to another - and too much of this would make the book unreadable - but I wanted to give a taste of what it is like in my head.

I first started thinking about why I wanted to write this book. I had to have a purpose, or else I wouldn't write anything and I wouldn't have anything to keep me motivated to type page after page. Once I knew why I wanted to write this book, I had to think about what information I wanted to include here - and then how best to structure that information.

In my mind, what came up was to write chapters in chronological order. There are some bits that didn't fit with this approach because they straddled many chapters, and other bits may get repeated but from a different perspectives. I decided that this was still the best approach to take - so that a parent with a young child with Asperger's or Autism Spectrum Disorder (ASD) can read that chapter and see what my experiences were as a child, and what I found helpful and not helpful at that age. Likewise, a parent of a child at a different age - or even someone with Asperger's - can look at the relevant chapter if that is what they are mainly interested in.

As well as having Asperger's Syndrome and being diagnosed as an adult, I have also worked with children of all ages with autism and Asperger's, both in residential childcare and together with families with children with autism and Asperger's. I have had experience of the system and supporting people through the system, and can share my experiences of trying to get diagnosis and help in England.

## Reason for writing this book

What motivated me to write this book was to give hope to parents of children with Asperger's and, indeed, to those with Asperger's Syndrome. I have worked with hundreds of parents over the last eight years, and during that time I have encountered many who seem to have no hope for the future of their child. They deeply love their child, with or without Asperger's, but many of them seem to believe that their child won't achieve much in life, because they have Asperger's.

I have worked with parents that use the term Asperger's as an excuse for their child's poor behaviour, and will sometimes say that their child has a genetic problem so they can't change: "This is the way they are, and so this is the way they always will be." These parents often don't try to address what can be done because they don't believe anything will work. They will respond to suggestions of what they could do by saying, "But that wouldn't work with my child, because he has Asperger's."

In the couple of years before I was diagnosed with Asperger's, I had been looking at myself and felt I most likely had Asperger's, but I didn't see the need to go through diagnosis to find out. I didn't see the need for a label. Generally, my view is that we are all human, and the one similarity all humans have is that we are all different. We all have our own unique set of skills and qualities. As time went on, a number of experiences led me to seek out diagnosis, and I'm glad I did.

Before I was diagnosed as having Asperger's I used to work with parents and would reframe their perspectives of what future their children could have by giving a different take on their children's traits, or - as I saw them - strengths. I remember teaching a parenting course, where a parent was saying that their child had Asperger's, and that he got so frustrated and angry; he struggled with socialising and didn't really have any friends. The mum went on to say she didn't hold out any hope for her son's future - she feared she would probably have to look after him well into adulthood. Even after that, he wouldn't be able to do any jobs as he would struggle with having work colleagues, and indeed anything where his routine may change. She said he

5

struggled to understand emotions, he always seemed emotionally disconnected and only ever seemed to get excited by noticing patterns in things. She said she knew he cared; he just didn't seem capable of showing it.

I responded by saying, "It sounds to me like he could make a great counsellor or therapist one day."

The mother looked at me, confused. Her background was in working with people with emotional difficulties in a school. I explained that, if he cared and wanted to help people, he would make a great therapist, because he wouldn't get sucked into all the emotions of the problem - something that many therapists do, and it clouds their perspective of a situation. He would be brilliant at picking out patterns in what was said, and at noticing the cause of the problem, and why a client would be stuck with it. I explained that many therapists get lost in the story the client tells, rather than being detached and noticing the patterns within the story.

The mother hadn't looked at her son's condition in this way before. She had said he was intelligent, so I commented that, as an intelligent person, he could learn many of the skills required to show empathy, and he could be taught when those skills should be applied. On the parenting course I was leading, I was teaching about I-messages and reflective listening - and this was with parents without Asperger's. I said, just as they were learning as parents how best to communicate, so could her son. (Her son was on the course in the young people's group learning these same skills and taking them in, despite the mother's insistence at the start that he probably wouldn't be able to. His favourite thing on the course was a relaxation technique which is a skill often vital for children with Asperger's.)

The mother smiled as her outlook for her son suddenly changed, and she saw hope for him. This also became a turning point for her and her son on the parenting course. She now had a more positive perspective on her son, and applications for his skills and abilities, rather than on his deficits and how he wouldn't achieve anything.

When I was sharing all this with the parent, I was able to do so congruently and with conviction, because I genuinely believed everything I was saying. I never told her - or any of the other parents - that I thought I had Asperger's. Rather, all I was doing was describing myself and some of my experiences as I will cover later in this book. Another reason for writing this book is to help me understand myself better. I have lots of information and views in my mind that I am always juggling. I decided that, if I wrote it all down, not only might it be helpful to others, but it might also help me to understand myself - to understand those aspects of myself I like, and those I'm not so keen on. It may also help me to understand how others see me, and how I annoy or irritate others unintentionally - and then what I could do about it.

Something I hope to achieve with this book is to show the development of my experience with Asperger's over the years. So, I hope to describe how I was at different ages - within this, many of the same symptoms will crop up repeatedly, but in different contexts. I hope that this will be helpful to parents with children with Asperger's; they may recognise some of the symptoms in their children, and they may as a result be able to see how their child's symptoms may progress, and how they may impact on their child growing up. It may even help parents to know what sort of advice or support to give to their child over the coming years, in order to minimise any negative impact.

## What is Asperger's (ASD)?

Asperger's is a collection of traits that Austrian paediatrician Hans Asperger recognised within children he was working with in the 1940's. The children appeared to have normal intelligence, but they struggled with non-verbal communication skills and didn't seem to show empathy to others. They spoke in an unusual way - often disjointed, with perhaps an odd pattern of speech, or they would speak in a very formal way, using full words and avoiding contractions (i.e., 'it does not' instead of 'it doesn't'). The children also seemed to have narrow and intense areas of interest - the only topics of conversation about which they wanted to talk.

It wasn't until 1992 that Asperger's Syndrome was used as a diagnostic term, and only in 1994 was it added to the fourth edition of the Diagnostic and Statistical Manual (DSM-IV). Asperger's has more recently been incorporated into autism spectrum disorder (ASD), as being on the 'high functioning' end of the autistic spectrum. To get a diagnosis, the psychiatrist or psychologist conducting the assessment will look to see whether the traits have been present since very early childhood, and will often want to talk to a parent or carer who can describe the birth and early years of the life of the person seeking diagnosis.

Asperger's is likely a genetic condition. There are some factors which may be related, like premature birth, and stress or illness during pregnancy. So, it is likely that someone with genetic susceptibility to Asperger's can have these genes activated by these factors. Asperger's is a lifelong, incurable condition that affects about 1 in 100 people.

Each individual with Asperger's will be affected in their own unique way. There are certain traits, but they affect each sufferer differently. Often, the key signs are: difficulties with social interactions (including difficulties understanding the behaviours of others), an intense and narrow interest on a topic, repetitive behaviours, and in childhood there could be delayed motor development or the child may exhibit clumsiness. Often, children with Asperger's will have developed linguistically and cognitively like normal - or perhaps even had advanced development in these areas.

As a child with Asperger's grows up, a parent may begin to suspect something is different about the child due to a lack of social interaction with other children. It is important to remember that Asperger's is a lifelong condition, so a child who had many friends in primary school and nursery school, but then stays in his/her bedroom and never socialises as a teen probably doesn't have Asperger's; on the other hand, a teenager who has never really had friends through their whole childhood, or perhaps latched onto just one or two friends through their childhood may be more likely to have Asperger's.

As a parent you would be looking for clusters of behaviours. Most traits aren't necessarily all present, but there are likely to be a number of traits expressed in some form or another. So the child may grow up with good speech, but all they do is talk about themselves, which is normal for young children, but which gets less common as children grow up. Alternatively, they may feel compelled to touch specific textures, or to avoid specific textures - or even specific sounds, sights, colours or smells. Their speech may be robotic, monotonous, or repetitive. They may struggle with using or understanding non-verbal communication, but may have very good verbal communication. They may not make eye contact, something many parents and teachers then try to teach the child to do - because most people are raised to look at someone when they are talking to you, as if somehow looking at someone makes the information go into the ears better.

People with Asperger's may well absorb what they are being told better if they aren't made to make eye contact. They may also struggle to understand social or emotional situations - they may find empathising difficult. This is also something that is normal for most teenagers at some point during their development, so it is important to look at this in context with any other signs you notice.

# CHAPTER TWO

## *Early Years*

Asperger's is a lifelong condition. To get a diagnosis of Asperger's the psychiatrist or psychologist carrying out the assessment looks to the past to see what the person undergoing the assessment was like in the early years of their life. Ideally, the psychiatrist wants to meet with the parents of the person being diagnosed; if that isn't feasible, they will want as much information as possible from different sources, to show what the person was like in those early years.

For me, my dad had unfortunately died from oesophageal cancer less than a year before my adult diagnosis. My mum, who lives some distance away, agreed to come to my assessment with me. If she wasn't able to attend, then they would have wanted to arrange a follow-up appointment at a time when she could attend - or at least to have a telephone appointment with her, although this wouldn't have been an ideal situation. So I was really glad that my mum was able to make it to my assessment; it definitely saved a lot of potential hassle and uncertainty that I wouldn't have liked.

When my dad died, I looked through many papers of his and found documents he had written about what I was like as a young child. He'd penned them when he was trying to get me seen by a medical professional, because he felt there was something wrong with me. I took copies of these with me to my assessment, and was glad I had these documents in case mum wasn't able to make it to the appointment with me.

If there is no-one to share what the person having the assessment was like as a small child (for example, if someone is going for an adult diagnosis of Asperger's Syndrome and either they were adopted or in care, or of an age where close family members have died), then getting this evidence can be more tricky. If the person seeking a diagnosis can get medical records - or has records from nursery school or play school - then this can be helpful when painting a picture.

In this chapter, I relate how my parents described me, and what I remember about being this young age. What I have noticed over the years is how rigid some elements of myself have been. I look back and see things at all different ages that I can still relate to now as an adult. It may be that you, the reader, have a young child, and as you read through this, you notice things that are similar in your child. It may be that you have Asperger's, or are thinking about whether you should seek diagnosis, and whether you are likely to discover you have Asperger's or not. You, too, may relate to some of these experiences.

Looking back, in hindsight, is often filled with connections and answers that were so easily missed at the time. Not only do I have this perspective, but I will also share some of my views from years of working with children with Asperger's and supporting parents of children with Asperger's, about what can be helpful and what I feel is unhelpful.

## Birth

I was born in the afternoon of 19th August 1978. It was a year and a few days after Elvis Presley had died of a heart attack in his bathroom. For most of my life, I have had an obsession with Elvis Presley's music and often wondered whether it is because his music might have been playing everywhere over the year after his death and I may have been listening to it through mum's womb, repeatedly picking up on it as something comforting.

This may sound odd, but there is research about music being played to babies in the womb - how such music can soothe the baby. The interesting thing is: if the child hears the music they heard while in the womb, they respond to it unconsciously; it evokes the emotional response they exhibited whilst in the womb. So, if a parent plays a specific calming tune into their womb repeatedly during pregnancy and the unborn baby responds with increased calmness, they can use that same music to help soothe and calm the child as they grow up; the child may well keep a positive association with that tune or music throughout their life.

This also works for voices. If a parent is often shouting and making the unborn baby experience repeated shocks each time they shout, and perhaps also scaring or unsettling their unborn baby, then this voice will have the same effect on the child as they grow up. The difference here is that they may become immune to the shouting and stop experiencing a shock sensation; instead, they may respond by just ignoring the shouting. If the parent regularly talks calmly and softly to the unborn baby and the voice soothes the baby, then that same voice will be likely to soothe the baby as they grow up.

I was due to be born in September 1978, but came out early. I was small but healthy. Mum has often told me that I never hugged her. I was my mum's first child so she didn't know what to expect. She didn't know what 'normal' behaviour was. If she tried to hug me, I would apparently push away. I have never really liked being hugged, but I do like to be tucked in tight sheets in a bed. Like much that I write about in this book, this is difficult to explain; once I start sharing things, they come out sounding like contradictions. That is one reason for writing this book - maybe, just maybe, seeing them in print will help me notice the connections, and I can then understand how they make sense, how they aren't as illogical as they seem.

I don't like the feeling of clothes wrapped around my arms, legs or neck, but I do like a t-shirt that is tucked in so that I can actually feel like I am wearing one. I don't like being hugged or having people getting close to me, but I do like to be in enclosed spaces or tucked into tight sheets.

When I was born, mum just assumed that my nan was picking me up and looking after me, and 'knowing better' when she was trying to help - that I perhaps was forming a closer attachment to my nan than my mum. Maybe that was why I didn't really hug her and why I would push her away, she thought.

My view is, if that was the case then I would have grown up being 'normal' about hugging, and it probably would have just been my mum that I didn't hug. In my ASD assessment, my mum described how I always shied away from being touched, and disliked being cuddled. Mum described how I was completely different to my other siblings. All of my brothers wanted hugs and attention from mum - and, in fact, other adults and children. I was happy to sit alone in a corner somewhere; I didn't feel a need to seek out the company of others.

One thing I remember from being very young is two teddy bears that I used to have. What I remember about them more than anything else is their smell and feel. One was a small yellow teddy bear with bristly fur. I remember rubbing the fur on my cheek and finding the feeling comforting. The other bear was softer and squishier. Both had different smells and both felt different, but both were comforting. I still own both of these teddy bears, although I don't think I have hugged them since I was just a few years old.

For any parent who can relate to what I have written about me as a baby, I wouldn't immediately jump to the conclusion that someone has ASD because they don't hug, or they push away, or because they were born prematurely. I would look at it as a possible indicator, if there are other things you notice about your child as they grow up. I think people seem to have a tendency to be very insular. They focus on themselves more than they realise. A parent in a similar situation with a baby that doesn't seem to be hugging them should look and see whether the baby is hugging other relatives to see whether the pattern is just with the mother, or also with other relatives and friends.

## Nursery school

I don't remember too much about nursery school. What stands out for me is having to stand on a bench in a small dimly-lit classroom singing 'ten sizzling sausages', and then having to jump off the bench when it got to my number. I know that even at this age I would rather be solitary. I was much more comfortable sitting on my own and looking through a book or pushing a singular toy around a room, usually a lorry or a train. I didn't like doing interactive or group activities, yet this is what everyone was pushed to do.

I remember mum telling me that when I went to my first day of nursery school, and on subsequent days, I walked straight in. I didn't hug mum goodbye, I didn't turn to see her before walking into to the nursery school, and I didn't cry. Mum told me, she thought at the time that this was a sign of positive attachment - that I must have felt secure in the knowledge that mum would be there when I came out of nursery school - so I was comfortable to go in without any problems. It is only over recent years, when looking back and reflecting, that she has said maybe it was a sign of something else.

I think this is an interesting one for parents, because I would be pleased with a child that doesn't cry at a school gate - a child who isn't clinging to me as a parent, who seems to be comfortable to just walk in to the school without any fuss - but obviously this is a rare reaction from most children. A healthy reaction would usually be perhaps anxiety about entering school on the first day, maybe anxiety, too, on a few subsequent days. After that, the child should have enough experiences of their time in school going well and their parent being there for them when they come out of school that they then begin to go into school without any hassle. It is unusual for this to happen straightaway.

From my perspective as the child, I didn't have a strong attachment to mum, or anyone else in my life, and unless I knew there was a reason to think differently, walking into one building was much the same as walking into another building. I'm sure many children with Asperger's would still find going into school something that evokes anxiety, something which may well lead to crying and may cause difficulty getting them to go in.

For me, I am generally a calm person. And think I always have been. So, in my early years - when I wasn't of an age where I had learnt about thinking about situations before being in them - I had no problem walking into situations. Most children gradually become aware of what others might think of them, and about how they may feel in a situation before they are actually there.

This lies at the heart of many issues that adults have; they have learnt to create mental images of what may go wrong in different situations. This then leads to anxiety, and can lead to avoidance, so that the anxiety or negative perceived outcome doesn't happen.

I am much like everyone else. I would rather avoid some situations than face the prospect of becoming anxious. My attitude to it is that, with many things, I decide I will do them despite feeling anxious, because if I don't, I would shut down much of my life. However, I do have coping strategies I use - especially in situations I have found myself in unwittingly, like being on crowded trains, or being in a town centre, or other locations where there are people around.

I remember in nursery school that I would keep myself to myself as much as possible, and would focus on one thing to shut out everything else. I don't know if this made me appear unresponsive at times, but I do know that I was often described as being a 'quiet, polite boy'. I wasn't intentionally being quiet or polite; I was just keeping in my own world. What I have learnt as an adult is the extent to which people are so self-centred - they often don't take the time to properly observe the external world. I didn't know that when I was just a young child, but I now know that this is likely to be the reason for people making interpretations like 'he is a quiet, polite boy'.

What they meant was: "He was quiet, so he must be a quiet boy, and because he was quiet when I was talking to him he must have been quietly listening, which is polite." It doesn't mean that my being quiet meant I was listening. I have experienced this in my adult life, too. People talk to me, I say nothing, and then weeks later they are telling me about how good it was to talk to me, how helpful my advice was. Yet, I never said anything... They did all the speaking and came to conclusions themselves.

## Toddler

I don't have many memories of being a toddler. I remember 'ten sizzling sausages' in nursery school, and I remember having a very heavy metal toy car that I'd sit in and pedal. I remember struggling to get it going. What I do have though is my dad's description of me that I hadn't seen until after he had died of cancer in 2014. A few days after he died, I was at home with my wife. We were going through old handwritten letters, when my wife found one dad had written that described me. She read it in silence for a minute first, and then said, "This describes you as you are now."

She started reading it out to me. It was a description of what I was like as a toddler. In the letter, dad was trying to get me an appointment with a doctor. He described how *'there is something wrong with Daniel'*. Much of this book's section on me as a toddler has used dad's descriptions as a starting point. When my wife read out these points I was instantly able to relate to many of them as things I still do, issues I still have, or things I have had into recent years but have gradually been working on reducing. With that in mind, many of these will crop up again in future chapters; I will expand on how they have manifested over the years, what impact they have had on my life, and what I have done about them.

When I was a toddler, I used to twitch. It wasn't a nervous twitch, but it was more something I felt compelled to carry out. I would also find myself tapping - tapping my feet, or tapping my fingers. To me, this wasn't a problem; it was something I did that was probably more of a problem to others than to me. I'm sure others used to find it annoying. I know this was the case later in life.

The whole time, while it isn't a problem to the person doing it and it isn't being identified as a problem by anyone else, there isn't any motivation to address it and change. I don't remember people telling me it was a problem to them until I was in secondary school. I didn't really try to do much about it until I was in my second job as an adult where people were identifying my tapping as a problem at work.

Something I found interesting when reading one of the letters my dad wrote was that I was mentally strange. I would seem to make connections in directions that seemed unusual or odd. To me, as an adult, I think of this as creativity. I can make some seemingly strange decisions. I also say things that now, as an adult, I know sound stupid; this doesn't stop me saying them and thinking they are perfectly natural, normal and logical at the time. An adult example of this is that if I meet someone who looks like someone else, I am very likely to ask them whether they know the person they look like. So far, everyone I have asked this has said they don't know the person. At the time I ask it doesn't seem odd; my brain says that if they look like someone else, then maybe they know them. It is only on reflection that I realise how ridiculous that sounds. It isn't like I think they are related to the other person - which could at least make some sense. I just seem to think that two similar-looking people must know each other.

I have three younger brothers; the next oldest is the son of my mum and dad, and the other two are my half-siblings. When my dad was describing what I was like as a child, he had my brother (two years younger than me) for comparison: him at that younger age and how I seemed to be at the older age. My brother apparently thought 'normally', whereas I had a different view of reality. This is a term I prefer now as an adult: that I have a different view, or perspective, on reality. It isn't that I have a problem; I just see the world differently. We all see the world differently to each other anyway, so this makes me more 'normal'. If I think of things as a bell curve, then the majority of people think similarly in the centre of the curve, and fewer and fewer people think similarly, the further from the centre of the bell curve you get. I would be towards one of the sides of the curve, but still somewhere on it - just like everyone else.

Another observation my dad made in his letter was that I had problems with reciprocal communication, and would only reciprocate if I was prompted and told what to say. This is again something that is still with me, except that as I have grown up, I don't respond so well to being prompted. As soon as I am prompted, I find myself not wanting to do what I have been prompted to do. I think, sometimes, that the person who prompted me will think I am only doing or saying what I then do or say because they told me to. This stops me doing it at all, which can, in turn, make me appear rude or ungrateful.

I definitely think my parents were correct in prompting me as a child. This has to be done with all children to a certain extent as they are learning and developing. I just never seemed to 'grow out of it'. I continue to this day to really need prompting, but unfortunately I don't respond as well as I probably did as a child to being 'told what to do'.

From a very young age, I started reading. From what I have been told, and what I can remember, I was very good at reading. Where I struggled was in relating to pictures in books. Most books for toddlers contain pictures to help the story along. For many children, the pictures in story books explain the story more easily for the child than the words do. Where I struggled was in identifying what was going on in the pictures. I couldn't grasp the emotions conveyed on characters that were drawn. If there was a picture of a child in a tree, I could say 'that child is in a tree'. If my parents asked "How is Billy feeling in that picture?", I wouldn't be able to read the drawing and work it out.

In his letters, my dad mentioned about issues he observed with my physical coordination as a toddler. When I was older, I definitely significantly improved in this aspect. Dad described that I wasn't clumsy, I just seemed to always bump into things as if I didn't recognise where parts of my body were. When I read this, I thought that described having a proprioception problem. I feel that this would fit with dad's description of me not being clumsy but having some kind of problem with my physical coordination. Likewise, from a young age, I have always been quite good at learning movements and climbing trees, and such things that children do. But I have always had a problem with the bits of me I can't see. When I was about ten years old, I cut my leg open falling over. This isn't unusual for a ten-year-old, except that I was standing still at the time and somehow managed to fall over just by moving a little.

Aged ten, I was climbing trees, cycling, horse-riding, playing tag, and so I definitely wasn't clumsy and always falling over and hurting myself. But still, I would often bash my legs or arms or shoulders or head into things, seemingly without realising it was about to happen.

As an adult, I was involved in a road accident which shattered my right arm. My right elbow now sticks out slightly further than it used to, and this slight difference means I am frequently banging it on things like door frames, because I seem to be unaware of its location in space. I also continue to knock my head and bash into things easily.

I remember mum always telling me that I was a bright child. I know this is what parents tell their children, but I do think I was intellectually bright as a child. I could understand what people meant when they told me things; even from a very young age, if I was told something clearly and logical - like telling me to carry out a task - I could do it. What I wasn't very good at was practical things. It took me a very long time to learn how to tie my shoelaces. I remember getting annoyed with myself because I couldn't do it. My brother, who is two years younger than me, was able to tie his laces before I could. I remember him making fun of the fact that he could tie his laces and I couldn't. This used to frustrate me. It made me more determined to succeed, so I would stop feeling like I was stupid.

The thing that frustrated me most was that I could understand the instructions about how to tie my laces. I could see laces being tied, and I believed I could copy the actions I had just watched. But when it came to doing it, I would fail. It didn't seem like it should be difficult, and this just made me more frustrated.

I remember being described as a child who was generally very calm and quiet. But I also threw tantrums. Every child throws tantrums from time to time, especially when they don't get their own way. I don't remember minding so much about getting my own way; I didn't care enough about most things to throw a tantrum about them. I was used to not getting my own way, because it led to a quieter life at home.

What I would throw tantrums about would be when plans were changed and we ended up doing something different to what we were supposed to be doing. Mum has described to me on occasions how I used to throw myself down on the ground and bang my head on the floor. She has described to me about how stubborn I would get at these times. I never liked change, and didn't cope well with it. If something changed, I had to know why, I had to know what the new plan was. I would ask lots of questions about what was going to happen, when and why. I would only calm down once I was happy with the answers to these questions.

In my assessment, mum described a time when she washed her hair and wrapped a towel around her head. I became upset because mum looked different to how she was before washing her hair and, to me, her hair looked 'messy' and I struggled to cope with this change. It is small changes like this that for most children are insignificant. A parent will wash their hair and carry on with the rest of their day. For mum, washing her hair could lead to a child throwing a tantrum and asking questions - she would have to deal with me wanting everything to go back to 'normal'.

As a child, dad described me as *'can be talkative, but talks endlessly about very little'*. I remember as a small child not really talking to people, whether it was friends, teachers, family or other adults, unless I had something I found interesting to say to them. Even then, it would be because they had instigated conversation. Many people saw me as a quiet child who didn't really say anything to anyone, and most of the time, this was the case. I think, through much of my life, people have mistakenly thought that I am shy, but the reality is that I don't really have any interest in most of what people talk about.

Dad would get annoyed with me repeatedly talking about the same subjects over and over again and not engaging in any other conversation. All my life I have described myself as being all or nothing. People will either struggle to get any communication out of me, or they will engage me in conversations about things I am interested in and I will talk at them about those things.

From as young as I can remember, mum always described me as being very grown-up in my way of talking and thinking. I quickly passed the stage of talking like a child. I didn't really do imaginative, make-believe talking. I could imagine and talk about ways of doing things, and would create things in my mind - like magic tricks. I could describe *them*, but this was using my imagination to create real-world items. I never really imagined in a fantasy way.

As well as talking a lot about very little, I used to *'repeat things like a parrot'*, as dad described me. I would copy words or phrases I heard that had a certain rhythm to them, or things that felt nice to say. I didn't consciously do this; I would just find myself doing it. It wasn't just speech that I would copy - I would copy sounds and tunes too. Again, to a certain extent, all children do this. I have always been fascinated by the scene in *Jaws*, when Martin Brody's son, Sean, is mimicking him at the dinner table. This is something most children do at some time as they grow and develop. I didn't copy body language like Sean was doing in *Jaws*, but I would mimic others verbally - and not directed back at the person I was mimicking. I wouldn't notice that I was mimicking; I would sometimes do it without any conscious awareness, other times I would become aware of what I was doing, but not of why. So I would know I was saying a phrase or word over and over again, but wouldn't realise that I was saying something someone else had said, and that I was actually copying them. Certain sounds feel good, and if I am absorbed in making them, then I am absorbed in that good feeling.

I always struggled to grasp ideas and concepts. Things had to be made clear for me to understand them. If something was too conceptual or too vague, then I would struggle to understand it or make sense of it. I have always been a very logical thinker, and so could figure things out. An example of this was when I was being babysat and the person looking after us children was sat on the sofa. His feet were gradually pushing the rug towards the fire. There was a fireguard to stop us going near and touching the fire, but the rug was pushing under the fireguard, and I could tell that the spitting fire from the crackling wood that was landing safely within the fireplace would end up going onto the rug and may have caused a fire. I reacted by pulling the rug away from the fire and making the situation safe.

Mum has described to me a few incidents like this, where I could analyse situations and work out that something could go wrong, and I would calmly make the situation safe. Like noticing that toast was being cooked and was burning, while the person cooking had forgotten about it. I knew to turn off the grill and remove the toast to stop it burning. I always seemed good at being able to logically and calmly work through situations in my mind and find solutions. I think it helped that I didn't really get emotional about things, so I didn't end up panicking and not knowing what to do.

I have always been described as a good eater because I will eat anything that is put in front of me and will eat everything. It is rare for me to leave food on my plate. What most people don't realise is how much I hate eating. This has been the case for as long as I can remember. I don't know for sure whether it has always been the case. Mum has always described me as a good eater. I know that, as a toddler, though, I didn't like eating, but rather I found eating a useful tool.

There are many children who seem to have a problem with being fussy about what they eat. My professional experience of this is that it is usually due to how parents have been around giving certain foods to their children. Either the child hasn't liked something so the parent has decided to offer something else, and over time this has become a pattern where the child has learned that they can react in a specific way and the parent will give them what they want, or the parent doesn't particularly like something, and the child picks up on their reaction to the food and adopts it.

Children are incredibly observant. They don't consciously realise how observant they are, but they can pick up on subtle communication from their parents. This is how children do all of their learning during the first few years of life. Most people who have sat through language lessons in school will know how difficult learning a language is. The teacher may well start by teaching how to count to ten, how to say who you are and how to say please and thank you. I know by the time I left school, having sat through lessons many times a week for five years, I still couldn't fluently speak French or German; yet, within five years of life, a child - who is just copying their parents and others around them - can speak their native tongue fluently, and they won't have had any formal lessons, partly because there is no language to use to teach the child.

So, if a child can learn an entire language to a level where they can hold conversations and be understood by the age of two, then they will have no problems learning other behaviours from their parents - like how they should behave during conflict, what foods they should and shouldn't enjoy eating, and how they should think about things.

What I found with eating, and still do, is that it gave me something to do in situations where others were around. I could focus on just eating and not be hassled into playing or interacting with others. So, eating in social situations can be protective; while you are eating, people assume you are doing something and are more likely to leave you alone. I would get comments about what a good eater I was, but people wouldn't focus on trying to get me to do something different instead of eating. Meanwhile, if I was sat quietly in a corner on my own, people would impose their own views and judgements on me and assume that I must be unconfident, or bored, or that I should go and play, and so they would try to push me into playing with others.

For as long as I can remember, I have never really noticed much about the taste of food - it has always been about how the food feels to eat. If the food doesn't feel right I will probably still eat it, but given the choice, I would always choose the foods that feel best to eat first. I like the feeling of chewing on juicy meat, or sloppy mash, or overcooked vegetables. I don't really like dry foods, like crackers or pastry. Eating is something I am often very indifferent about, so as a child, if food was placed in front of me, I would eat it. On the other hand, if there was no food, unless I was very hungry or in a situation where food would save me from interacting with others, I wouldn't see a need or have a desire to eat.

Something I have always struggled with when eating is how to eat without biting the inside of my mouth. My whole life, this has been an issue, Somehow, probably fifty percent of the time I eat, I will end up biting the inside of my mouth - my cheeks, or my lips, sometimes even my tongue. I do it less when I focus solely on eating and I ignore everything else so that I can picture in my mind where the food is in my mouth at any given time and carefully track its movements during each chew.

Probably the most obvious area to parents of a child on the autistic spectrum is how their child plays and interacts with other children, or - more likely - how they don't seem to be playing or interacting with other children. This was definitely a feature of my childhood. My dad described how I didn't seem to be able to grasp that play was fun, and that I didn't seem to play with others.

For me, play was more of a practical and solitary thing, especially in my early years. If I received Lego, I would sit quietly and diligently making what was on the box, following the instructions. I would rarely make something different with the Lego. I was happy to put together a train track from a wooden train set and just push the train around the track, but wouldn't play with others. When I did play with others, it would either be because it was being forced upon me, or because I was carrying out a specific role. So, I could be playing a game with someone else, like my brother, and we would both have roles to play in the game. He may be playing the King during a game, and I may have to collect things for him, and so I would go off on my own and collect things and return them, but we wouldn't actually be playing together: I would be doing my thing and he would be doing his.

It was always really difficult to understand play, because people would say that one thing was actually something else as if it actually was something else, and then they would treat it as that other thing. So they may, say, use kitchen roll tubes as swords and act like they really were swords, even though I knew they weren't - they were just kitchen roll tubes. Someone saying 'let's get in the car' and then getting in between some cushions from the furniture placed around the floor and pretending to drive off and perhaps pretending to evade a chasing car was always confusing to me. Some things made more sense though: someone saying 'let's hide in the den', and then getting in under a blanket propped up by cushions, for example, made more sense, because we had made that den. It was a static object with walls and a roof.

If you are a parent reading this and you recognise in your child a lot of what I have written about as a toddler and from my nursery school experiences, then they may well have autism spectrum disorder (ASD). Everyone's experience on the autistic spectrum is different, but there will also be similarities. A child with ASD will have issues socially, they will view life quite literally rather than metaphorically and they are likely to have sensory issues. In the next chapter, I will be discussing what I was like through my primary school years. This is the first period of my life where I can confidently recall memories. During the chapter, I will cover how my experiences developed as I grew up.

If your child is displaying similar behaviours to those I have described here, it may be worth talking with a general practitioner about whether an ASD assessment would be worth looking into. As a general rule, I'm not a fan of labelling people, but I am aware that if someone is in need of additional support, then a label can be useful. For example, having an ASD diagnosis can help get extra support around education. Adults with ASD can also get extra support within their work. I wish I had been diagnosed younger, as I believe it would have helped me over the years.

Dan Jones

# CHAPTER THREE

## *Primary Years*

Many of my earliest memories are from my primary years. I don't really remember much before that, and what I *think* I remember, I can't be confident about - are they my memories, or just memories based on photographs I have seen? In this chapter, I will share my experience of my primary school years from about five years old up to ten or so. During this time, I began to recognise that I was different and started to learn about how to cope with the world around me.

Mum always described me as having a lot of common sense. I would describe myself as having common sense that sometimes isn't common, and other times doesn't make sense... From a very young age, mum trusted me to look after my younger siblings. She had tried babysitters, but often I was still the person with the most common sense in the room. I had good observation skills for safety, and because I couldn't care less about most things that others seemed to really care about, I was often very calm. If there was an incident that needed to be handled I was likely to be the one who could work out what to do, and then calmly do it. This trait has helped immensely throughout my life.

Mum was a riding instructor, so growing up, she had to work when everyone else was off. My stepdad was a landscape gardener, so he worked long hours whenever the weather was suitable. Because mum taught people to ride horses, I spent most of my time around horses as a child. From the age of about eight, when mum was teaching, I would often be looking after my brothers. We would be at the riding centre, so mum wasn't far away if we needed her - she couldn't afford to have anyone else look after us, but she trusted me and felt I was responsible enough to look after my brothers. I knew that if there was a problem, I could either find mum, or seek out any of the other adults who ran the stables.

I remember some of my first experiences attending my first primary school. It was a small school with a cold outdoor swimming pool. I have certain memories that stand out about the pool. I remember flies floating in the pool. I remember the smell of the water. It smelt like water - I mean, it didn't have an odd smell - but I remember the fresh watery smell from the pool. I also remember the feeling of being in the water, and remember times when my nan would come along and help out during swimming lessons. I didn't like the swimming cap I had to wear. It used to hurt my head when I put it on and took it off. The cap would stick to my hair and felt like it pulled hair out of my head whenever I took it off. I did enjoy swimming though. My favourite thing about swimming was being underwater. I loved putting my head underwater, and as I got more confident, I would hold myself fully underwater at the steps. I loved how the sound changed underwater - it was quiet and peaceful, not as chaotic and overwhelming as the world above the water. I remember believing I could almost breathe underwater. I was aware that I couldn't, but I felt that I was able to stay underwater longer by relaxing and imagining I was breathing, so I would make all the actions of breathing without actually breathing in. I would almost cycle air round, as if I was somehow breathing within myself.

I didn't really have many friends in primary school. I was polite, so if someone engaged with me, I would be polite and do my best to try to engage with them back, but I didn't really have much interest in interacting with other people. I would much rather have spent a break time at the hedges around the outside of the school grounds searching for snails and looking at other creatures. I didn't feel like I was missing anything. I would take an ice cream tub around with me which I would fill with leaves, twigs, snails, caterpillars or grasshoppers. I wasn't necessarily very good at socialising, and didn't particularly care about others. That isn't to say I wanted bad things to happen to others - I have always wanted everyone to be alright - but I was far more caring of animals. One day, when I was out with mum while she was teaching horse riding, I found an injured grasshopper. I took it home and tried to nurse it back to health by creating an environment for it and giving it some food. Unfortunately, it didn't survive. I didn't get upset about it not surviving. I wanted it to live and get better, but my attitude was: once it had died, it had died. I did all I could think of to try to save it, and to my knowledge I couldn't have done more. I remember burying it in the garden, because I thought that was what was supposed to happen to dead things, then I got on with my life. I didn't get upset about not being able to save it, because I had done everything I felt I was able to do.

At one time, mum tried to arrange a birthday party for me at home. She invited many children I knew, and on the day of my party, no-one turned up. I think this was a telling sign of my relationships with others. I was polite to people but never really invested in my relationships with the other children in school. I was pretty much the same at home. I would prefer to spend time alone doing my own thing, but was generally polite. I don't recall too much play with my brothers. When we did play, it was usually something active like hide and seek or manhunt, or it was making dens or climbing trees. It wasn't really things where I was having to play with my brothers, but more things where I played alongside my brothers, or could feel like I was doing my own thing or engaging in a project - making something for some purpose.

I was far better at getting on with adults. I would ask questions all the time about things I was interested in, wanting to know more. At school, I would take my time getting ready to leave lessons so that the other children would leave and I could then ask the teacher any questions I had. If the lesson didn't interest me, then I would get out as quickly as I could to try to avoid being stuck in the middle of a crowd of children all leaving at once. If I had to choose between spending time with children or adults I would usually choose to stand around the adults, and would normally latch on to one adult whom I would sit next to and talk to. That adult was normally chosen because they'd first approached me and started talking to me, but they would then be stuck with me until they walked away. If they walked off and left me, I wouldn't seek anyone else out; I would rather sit on my own and keep myself to myself. Sometimes, another adult would come and talk to me and I would then talk to them about topics I enjoyed until they walked off too.

Before I really discovered non-fiction books, my favourite thing to play with was Lego. I would like making what was on the box - most of the Lego I had was normal Lego, but I always asked for Technic Lego for birthdays and Christmas - it looked and sounded more grown-up, and my view was, with Technic Lego, you were making something proper, not just a brick house or an equally simple item. I remember getting a Lego train set one year. I loved the feel of the train rails - how smooth they were on top - and loved how they fitted together and the smell of the pieces. I also loved the feel and smell of Lego tires. I would put them in my mouth and gently squish them between my teeth just to get the feeling of them.

When I used my Lego, I would place parts in orderly piles on the floor, and would get annoyed if anyone knocked them and messed up my area. I have mentioned previously - and will probably mention again - that things I say seem to have a lot of contradiction in them, which is confusing to me. However, I see these areas of contradiction and confusion as places where I am likely to learn more about myself. One such area is how I like things to be tidy and to make sense, yet I can easily live in a mess. My Lego on the floor probably looked messy, but I would have everything in its place. I would know where all the different kinds of blocks were. There would be order to my mess. As a child, especially, I found that I could focus on one thing, and that what mattered to others didn't necessarily matter to me. Mum often said she thought I would grow up to be a mad professor, always coming up with ideas and creating inventions but living in a mess. I don't remember thinking of my bedroom as a mess - things would be in piles where I could find them.

I did sometimes play team games, but I never volunteered to play - rather, it would be because I was told I had to play. Just like in school, when children are told they have to play football. I'm not totally against playing team games, I just don't focus on the team element of the game. I remember in my second primary school, a very small school in Arundel, West Sussex, playing football from time to time with other children, because many of them enjoyed football, and the only way to fit in was to join in. I have always liked being very active, so I liked running around. I liked being chased by people and seeing if I could evade them. But I didn't like having to be part of a team and having to interact with others. What's more, I didn't care whether I won or lost, which didn't seem to go down well with others on the same 'team' as me.

My focus was on questions like: 'I wonder whether I can make it to the other end of the pitch without anyone getting the ball off of me...' I didn't care whether they could or not. I would just want to find out the answer; and then next time, I would try to do better than my previous times.

I remember one football game where my thinking got me in trouble. One advantage of not particularly being interested in others and treating everyone about the same, regardless of who they are and what they are like, is that I would blend into the background and fit into most groups. There have always been exceptions, but generally I could loiter with a group and no-one would question my presence - sometimes, people wouldn't even be aware that I was there. One day while playing football on the playground in my primary school, the ball was kicked by someone. It left the playground and rolled down the grass bank alongside the playground.

Down the bank, two children got hold of the ball and started to throw it between them. Another child and I went down to get it back. When we got near the children, the other boy went closer to get the ball. He got between them, and they started throwing the ball over his head to each other. I got close to them but was stood off to the side - almost like myself and the two children were in a triangle. One of the children said 'here', and threw the ball to me. I caught the ball, turned around, and started walking back to the playground.

At that point it didn't cross my mind that they were including me in their 'game' of throwing the ball over the head of the other child, and that they didn't actually want us to have the ball back. I just thought it was thrown to me to take back to the playground. I walked towards the playground and back up the grass bank, when one of the children jumped on me angrily. I had no idea why they were angry and why they jumped on me. Then, one of the children playing football shouted at that child and jumped on him, then the other child jumped on to that child, and another child who was playing football jumped on them, and then it seemed nearly all the boys in the playground got involved.

I calmly crawled out from under the pile of children, walked across the playground, still holding the ball, and told a teacher that a fight seemed to have started down the grass bank. I didn't think any more of it. Some teachers dealt with the situation, and break time ended.

The next morning in assembly, the Head Teacher spoke about the fight that happened in the playground the day before. He said he wanted the children who started it to stand up. About six children stood up. He then said the person who was the main cause of the fight hadn't stood up, and he wanted him to stand up as well. I looked around wondering who it was. As far as I could see, the children that had taken the ball had both stood up - as had the children that attacked those two, when one of them had jumped on me.

After what seemed like a long pause, the Head singled me out and told me to stand up, saying I was the cause of the fight. This confused me; all I'd done was go and get the ball and walk back up to the playground with the ball, and then, when a fight broke out, I'd gone and got a teacher to deal with the fight. I remember being annoyed for ages about being blamed for something I felt I hadn't done.

Every year, as a young child, our family went on holiday to local holiday camps. One year while on holiday at a local camp, my brother and I were signed up to learn and play football with West Ham football players. My brother appeared to love it, and played well. I, on the other hand, didn't. I didn't want to play football. I didn't care that it was apparently professional football players teaching us - despite being told that I should care and that it was a great opportunity. My stepdad got very angry about me refusing to play football and join in the football lessons he had paid for. He was saying how he had paid for us to do it, and we should be grateful and keen to do it - it is what boys do and what boys like. My view was that I didn't ask him to pay for me to play football. I didn't say I wanted to play football, so why would I play football? It wasn't my problem he had spent his money on it - to me, that didn't change anything. Telling me he spent money on it, or that I should take part, wasn't going to change anything. I still wasn't going to play.

What I wanted to do on holiday was to go to the beach, and to play on my own, or go swimming in a pool on my own. I used to dislike having to spend enforced time with my brothers and family, so the last thing I would want to do was to spend enforced time in the company of football players and groups of other highly active and chaotic children. I have always preferred peace and calm over chaos and sensory overload.

The first primary school I attended was in Aldingbourne, West Sussex. I was there until I was seven. The family then moved from Westergate to Warningcamp, a small town a few miles away, on the outskirts of Arundel. There, I went to a primary school in Arundel, before attending secondary school in Littlehampton.

While I was at primary school in Aldingbourne, I began reading books. I remember lessons where teachers would read stories like *The BFG* and *Stig of the Dump*, and we would sit on the floor and listen to the stories being read. I used to listen to these stories being read and think that they didn't sound like the stories we had available to us to read. I didn't really understand why I had to read these books. I read them, but they didn't really interest me. They were so small and easy to read that by the time I left the primary school, I had read every book available to me. My reading age had been measured at the end of my final term in the school when I was seven; I was identified as having a reading age of at least nine and a half.

I didn't really enjoy reading the fiction books I was made to read. My favourite fiction books were those where each chapter ends with different options and you have to pick an outcome for the chapter and read from the page number for the chosen outcome. For books like that, I used to like trying to work out which option was likely to have the most beneficial outcome, and why. The books were always mystery books, so I used to try to look through the chapters to notice any clues - either in the writing or in the images - that would give me more knowledge about which option I should select.

I don't recall seeing any non-fiction books until I was eight years old. Prior to that age, the only books I was aware of were very thin and uninteresting children's books. It was shortly after starting my second primary school that I became aware of other books and genres.

Not long after starting in the school, the Head Teacher at the time was clearing out old books. I knew my grandparents had old books, but I had never looked at them; we had some old books at home, too, but I hadn't looked at those either. But in school we were told that we could look through the books and see if there were any we would like to keep. Obviously, I, like any other child, wasn't going to want to miss out, so I took a look at the books.

I still own almost all of the books I picked up on that day. One or two have gone missing over the years, but may turn up one day. The first thing I noticed about the books was the age of some of them. Some dated back to the 1800s, which I found exciting - to be able to hold and read something from that long ago. To me as an eight-year-old, these books that were over 100 years old were fascinating. They were older than any people I knew. I was able to hold something that people had held and read a century earlier. I still love old books, and for some reason, my definition of an old book is still one that is dated 1899 or earlier - even though I am thirty years older now than I was as an eight-year-old. I don't think of books from the 1900s as old, even though, now, a book from 1929 would be as old to me now as a book from 1899 was to me then.

The second thing I noticed about all these old books - and it still wasn't the content of the books - was their smell. I loved the smell. There was, and still is, something calming about the smell of an old book. Third was the feel. They didn't feel like the school books I was used to handling, with their glossy pages. The feel of things is very important to me. I don't mind the feel of a new glossy book, and don't mind the smell of new glossy books - but nothing compares to the feel or the smell of old books.

That day in school, I picked up many books about geography, physics, poetry - and even some novels, like *20,000 Leagues under the Sea*, and *Gulliver's Travels*. During my primary school years, I was bought many non-fiction books. At my second primary school I had stopped reading fiction books altogether, because I couldn't see the point in them when nothing they taught was real.

The last fiction book I read, other than *Z for Zachariah* and *Macbeth* in secondary school (which we were made to read as part of our English lessons), was a hardback collection of *Secret Seven* stories which mum gave me one day when I was home ill from school, aged eight.

At about the same age, I found a book that had a profound influence on me - *The Magic of Thinking Big*. This was a book I found lying around the house one day, and as a small child who loved magic, seeing a book with 'Big' and 'Magic' both written in the title was enough to make me want to know what it was about. The book taught me that you can achieve almost anything; you just have to plan and put in effort.

I learnt an incredible amount between the age of eight and ten - it has helped me immensely. The next significant learning wasn't until I was 13, when I discovered hypnosis. As well as discovering *The Magic of Thinking Big*, I also lived in an environment that allowed me to spend a lot of time in the woods - or at least outside, with nature. I used to spend much of my time sitting in trees. I found life at home often stressful and noisy, and I wanted to escape, so I would go into the woods. I would find a tree, climb up high, and sit on a branch with my eyes closed, just listening.

In the tree I would focus my attention on the sounds of birds. I would try to locate where they were by focusing on individual sounds. I would focus on the sounds of the rustling leaves and try to notice each individual one, trying to break the sound down and see how it was formed. As an eight-year-old, I had never heard of meditation, but I had discovered meditation for myself. Sitting in a tree doing this helped me to feel calm; it helped to shut out the 'noise'. I think I was lucky having the opportunity to grow up in the countryside rather than in a town during this period of my life. Warningcamp became a place I would call home as a child - and still think of as home now.

Having a mum who was a riding instructor also gave me the opportunity to be around horses for all of my childhood. Mum has always told me I seemed to have a natural talent for horse-riding. I think I just feel a closer connection to animals than I do to people. Animals don't expect me to try to communicate with them verbally - they don't communicate with multiple messages, like people do. Most animals communicate very simply. People can say one thing and mean something else, and then when you don't understand that they meant something else, they get annoyed or they tell you that you are stupid for not realising or understanding. On the other hand, an animal will just communicate one message at a time.

I used to have no problem getting on to any horse and riding it - horses seemed to trust me, as I did them. That doesn't mean I thought they would never hurt me, but what I trusted was that they would be clear with their messages, and that I would understand them. Most wild animals, and many other animals, don't demand my attention. I like being in nature, just observing, rather than needing to play with the animals. I love observing and learning, and it was this mindset which helped me to discover meditation sitting in the trees. All I was trying to do was to observe and learn. In the same way that someone parking a car may turn the music down to help them park, I closed my eyes to help me hear and focus.

During these early years, I started to become aware of patterns. I don't know whether I had always liked patterns, but I was becoming more self-aware and so becoming more aware of what I liked and didn't like. I seemed to have an ability to guess well with competitions like 'how many coins are in the jar'. At a country fair, when I was about eight, I guessed the number of coins in a jar and got it correct. During the summer holidays when I was nine or ten, myself - along with many other children from the two primary schools in Arundel - painted a mural of different animals. On the last day, we were told to guess how many animals were on the mural, and the person who guessed closest would win a prize to be presented by the Mayor of Arundel. I guessed closest - just one number out.

Many of my lifelong interests started between the ages of five and ten. I have always been confused by people changing tastes and interests as they grow up. My view is that if you like something, why would you one day not like it? Between five and ten, I developed an interest in the music of Elvis Presley; I discovered books that taught me things, rather than just being stories; and I started meditating, although I didn't know it was meditation at the time. I also became aware of some of my habits which would sometimes get me in trouble.

If I heard tunes or sounds, I would make the same sound myself, usually whistling it. I would copy words or phrases that people said which, for some reason, resonated in my mind when I heard them. What's more, I would often copy them in a replication of the person's voice. I didn't realise that mimicking people could offend them - it would just happen automatically. I didn't even realise I was mimicking them. And when I became aware I was saying or doing something, like whistling or saying a phrase in a specific way, I didn't normally know where it came from or why I was saying it - it would just happen.

I would find myself mimicking accents and speech patterns that seemed to resonate with me. The best way to avoid offending people was to avoid people, to try and keep my mouth shut, and to keep what went through my head in my head. This was never easy, as most of what I would do would just happen. Often others would point out to me what I was doing, and I found it very difficult to stop something when I didn't notice myself doing it.

Mum has always described me as being very academic. Whereas my brothers would want to go out and play games and play with toys, I was more focused on wanting to read books and learn. From a very young age, we had televisions in our bedrooms as children. Over my early years, I shared a room with each of my brothers. When I was between five and nine or ten years old, I shared with my brother - who is two years younger than me. He liked to go to bed early and liked playing team games; he always wanted to be competitive. I was totally different. I didn't really want to play with him or anyone else, and definitely didn't want to play competitive or team games. I like to do the best I can, but I don't care whether I win or lose - and, with that in mind, I don't like playing with people who are very competitive and get angry if they are losing, and over-excitable and smug if they are winning.

We both liked different TV programmes. Every year, around Christmas time, the *James Bond* and *Jaws* films would be on different TV channels at the same time. My brother always wanted to watch *James Bond*, I always wanted to watch *Jaws*. Not because it is supposed to be a scary film, or a gory film - although I have always liked horror films because they can make me jump and can evoke feeling in me. I wanted to watch *Jaws* because it has many nature scenes to watch and listen to, and footage of sharks and fish, which I find relaxing. *James Bond*, meanwhile, seemed to be all about people interacting with each other - there were very few slow scenes of nature. It also had far more loud music and sounds like gunshots.

It's not that I don't like *James Bond* - I like clever action scenes, inventions and ingenuity - but given the choice, I will watch the film with the most nature. Not that any film was particularly easy to watch back in those days, when I would be trying to watch the film on a black and white screen smaller than a mobile phone, embedded within a briefcase-sized box, with a fuzzy picture and having to constantly move the aerial around in the room trying to hold it in the perfect position for the duration of the film...

One thing I discovered from having a television in my bedroom was Open University TV programmes. Late at night, after my brother had fallen asleep, I would often watch the TV on quiet because I was still wide awake. Eventually, I noticed there were programmes on that seemed to teach things like maths and science. It didn't matter too much what the topic was - these programmes were educational. They weren't just wasting my time. I didn't always understand what I was learning, but I enjoyed watching them because I felt, for the duration of the programme at least, that I was learning something and could follow what was being taught. I never felt like I didn't understand.

When I was eight, I remember mum taking me to Arundel library. She knew how much I loved learning. Mum got my brother and me library cards. When I went in, I sat down on the floor and read many of the non-fiction books in the children's section. The books in the children's section didn't really take much time to read. I was able to withdraw many books at once, so I quickly worked through all of the children's non-fiction books that I was interested in. One day, not that long after joining the library, I wanted to go into the adult section. I could see there were so many more books in the adults' section. The librarian told me I couldn't go in because I was a child. I tried to explain that I wanted to read the adult books, but she refused to allow it.

This frustrated me. I couldn't understand why I wasn't allowed to learn what adults were. Growing up, it was common for my brothers and me to get bought a mix of toys and books for Christmas and birthdays. My brother didn't usually want the books he was bought - he found them boring - and I usually didn't want the toys I was bought, for the same reason. So we would swap with each other. I would give him my toys and he would give me his books. One year, when I was ten, an uncle of mine, who was a magician among other things, gave me an A-level book on science. I remember my mum instantly taking it from me. She was aware it was a book for someone older than me. She said to me that my uncle didn't really understand children - he didn't know what you should get children of my age for presents. She told me she would return it to him and see if he could get me something more suitable.

49

I didn't want 'something more suitable' - I wanted that book - so I kept the book. I remember reading and re-reading it, and carrying it around with me everywhere. When I was older, ideas in the book got me in trouble in school in science because I was giving answers that were different to the answers I was 'supposed' to give. This science book was the first of many science books I have been bought, and purchased myself, over the years. It became common to get science books - or books on general knowledge or nature or dinosaurs - for birthdays and Christmases.

## Magic, misdirection and friendship

Although during my primary years, I had poor emotional connection. I didn't really notice it. From my perspective, I was living in my own world. My dad had written about my poor emotional connection, and mum has mentioned my difficulties with emotional connection, but to me, I was more interested in doing things on my own. Human nature is a wonderful thing, although I didn't approach others to try to befriend them. Others would sometimes approach me; I liked familiarity and certainty, and I disliked engaging with people. I think I was lucky in some of my early 'a-ha' moments!

One such moment was realising that if I had a friend or two, I felt more comfortable speaking with them than with people I didn't know. I was able to learn how they would respond, and if they walked away and stopped spending time with me, it wasn't important - but while they were there, I could use them to make my life more comfortable. Writing this down here with my 'adult head' on, I feel like it sounds bad. It was, and still is, one of my ways of coping with the world.

If I wanted something, all I had to do was find a way of getting the person I was friends with to be the one to sort it out. So, if I wanted to have something to drink I would try to think about how I could encourage my friend to go to a teacher and ask for me. I would do things like encouraging them - saying that it would be good if we could both have a drink - or I would appear to be helpful and if we were doing something together, like making something, I would offer to do a task I thought they would least like to do. I'd say, "I'll do this if you want", and while they are pleased with me doing something they didn't want to do, I would say something like, "This is quite difficult, would you be able to grab me a drink?" I would try to make it look like I didn't want to stop then, because I was so focused on getting it done - I'd get the message across that what would really help me to get things done was having a drink...

As an adult, I now know that I was playing into a theory from social psychology about how people like to reciprocate - if you do something for someone, they are more likely to do something in return. Between about eight and ten years old, I learnt a number of these techniques to influence situations and to make them more comfortable for me. Then, in later life, when I discovered hypnosis, I realised that many of these techniques are in fact hypnosis techniques. Another technique I used to use was one for influencing groups of people. When I was in the playground and would want to play manhunt, for example, and everyone else was thinking about playing football, I would suggest the idea of manhunt loudly enough for the children either side of me to hear the idea, I wouldn't make a big deal out of it. After a moment or two, if those children quite liked the idea, they would suggest it, and gradually the idea would spread through the group, until the children who actually made the decisions picked up on the idea. Then, one of them would suggest it, and everyone would agree with the person who suggested the idea. No-one would realise that I had suggested the idea first, and I didn't care whether I got credit for the idea or not - as long as we were doing as I wanted.

I saw this happen to other children, where they would suggest ideas, seemingly get ignored, then eventually someone else would suggest the same idea and everyone would agree with that person; the child who originally suggested the idea would get stroppy about how they had come up with the idea first. It confused me as to why they got stroppy when they were doing exactly what they wanted to be doing. Did it really matter who took the credit for the idea?

This idea didn't always work - not all my ideas were things that everyone wanted to do - but if I was expected to play with other children, I would rather do something I see as having educational value than just, say, playing football. I liked manhunt because I got to practice evading capture, I developed skills for sneaking around and having patience. I could see that these skills could have value. I couldn't see how chasing a ball and hitting it into a net had value. You also don't have to work with others when playing manhunt. You may share a team, but you still work on your own, whereas with football you are expected to work together.

I have never been particularly competitive, but I do like to do the best I can - and I stick to rules. I don't have a very good emotional connection with others and struggle to understand their perspectives on many emotional issues. Mum and dad have both described how I seemed to have poor emotional connection. I have learnt over the years how I am supposed to respond in some situations. I still make mistakes, but I do much better than I did when I was young.

I remember playing manhunt while at a scout camp. All the scouts were divided up into two teams, with a few leaders on each side. I had been evading capture through most of the game, when one of the scout leaders noticed me and gave chase. The idea of the game was for the other team to touch you, and you were 'out of the game'. As the scout leader followed me through the woods, I jumped over and ducked under branches, evading him. Then, as I jumped over a fallen tree, the scout leader ran straight into it, breaking his leg and collapsing on the floor. He screamed in pain and asked me to help him. I went back to him and stood near him - but out of his reach - and shouted for someone to come and help him. I wasn't prepared to get close enough to be touched, because that would put me out of the game. Once I saw others coming I ran off and disappeared into the woods.

From my perspective, I did what I could to help without getting tagged. From the perspective of others, they felt I should have stayed and helped more and stopped the game at that point because someone had been injured... But if I had stopped and helped and been touched, I would have been out, had they decided to continue with the game.

I recall as a child regularly being told off for answering for my brother. Mum would be driving along and would ask my brother what the road sign coming up said. Before my brother had time to answer, I would pipe up for him. I don't know why I did this, and I know I still do it. When it happens is confusing to me. If I am on a training course, I don't do it, because the trainer is the perceived expert and I am not there to show what I know, I am there to learn. In other situations, though, like watching a film or television programme, I can't help myself. An example would be watching *The Mentalist*. This is one of my favourite TV shows and I usually know who is likely to have been the murderer - and how and why it happened - even before the titles roll at the beginning of the programme. The same with *Elementary*, and often *Sherlock*, and magician programmes like Derren Brown's shows - and his live shows too. When I know the likely answer I feel compelled to tell people my theory. Whenever I come up with ideas, I always feel compelled to share them.

Mum has always told me that I have a natural talent for music. As an adult, I can't play any musical instruments - although I love the idea of being able to play them, and so have many different instruments I one day hope to play, and I do try to learn. But as a young child, I was better at some aspects of music. When I was about six or seven, my nan taught me to play *Yellow Bird* on the piano, which I can still play, and my grandad taught me to play a few two-handed songs: *In The Mood* and *Sentimental Journey* with a left-hand boogie-woogie shuffle. My hands were initially too small, but I picked it up and grasped it quickly from copying what my grandparents had showed me. I had difficulties synchronising my left and right hands while playing, but didn't do too badly given I hadn't really played anything on a piano before, and had never had any music lessons.

Unfortunately, my stepdad didn't like us playing music at home, so I only ever got to play instruments when I was at my grandparents' house - even then, I had my brothers around, so didn't really have much chance to properly learn instruments. I remember sitting at nan and grandad's piano for hours at a time trying to play tunes, following the *Learn Piano* books. I could get through all of the books and play everything slowly, but I could never seem to progress to playing faster and more fluidly.

During my primary years, I remember finding it difficult to relate to others. No-one around me seemed like me. I felt I was different to everyone else in my life. To some extent, I felt my grandad was similar - he always seemed calm and everything about him seemed logical. He was interested in playing music and cycling, and worked as an accountant. He didn't display lots of affection by hugging, and gave minimal interactions with others from what I could see as a child. Also, one of my uncles played the trombone and loved trains, even working on the railway - but he also seemed to like more social interaction. He seemed to want to be in the company of others, even though he also appeared nervous or shy around other people. The family member who most interested me was one of my uncles. Among other things, he was a magician. He also designed things like irrigation for golf courses, and had an interest in photography. I remember always being fascinated by his magic tricks. He also set puzzles for me in birthday and Christmas cards, to which I would reply with puzzles back to him.

I have always loved magic. Unlike some people, who don't want to know how things are done, my mindset is that I want to know; knowing doesn't detract from the experience of the trick from me. It is the process of the trick and how it was done that I like, more than the end result - even for tricks with simple methods. I often hear people say that the solution to some tricks is so simple, that knowing it would ruin the trick. But when I see a card disappear and I have somehow not noticed how it was done, I want to know how it worked. I know the magician must have palmed the card, but I didn't see it, so I want to know the technique they used - if the card is to appear elsewhere, or to change into another card, or there is some other element to the trick, I want to know this too.

When I used to watch my uncle, he wouldn't tell me how his tricks were done, so I wanted magic sets and books on magic for presents. I would fill notepads with ideas about how different tricks could be performed. One trick I designed in a notepad was an escapology trick, where a heavy weight would be lifted into position by a crane, carefully positioned on four poles (one in each corner) above a box which has the magician in. Each pole is attached by a long chain to a car, so there are four cars facing diagonally away from the box. Once the chains are attached, the cars accelerate away from the box, with the chains being just long enough to pull tight after exactly 30 seconds. Once this happens, the poles get pulled from under the weight and it falls on the box. The 'trick' is for the magician to escape the box before the weight falls. This obviously doesn't happen… The box falls, explosions happen around the box and a cloud of smoke hides the box for a moment, then as the smoke clears, the magician is standing on top of the weight in a 'success pose'.

I used to perform magic tricks for my uncle whenever I knew he would be visiting my grandparents. I wasn't very good at dexterous magic tricks, like card tricks, but I often used to put on little shows, consisting of a range of memory tricks, some card tricks and disappearing item tricks. My favourites were escapology tricks. I used to like figuring out how to escape from different situations. One of my brothers had the misfortune of being my assistant in a box during my 'stabbing canes through a box' trick. I would ask him to climb into a box, seal the lid, and then stab canes through the box as quickly (and accurately) as I could. Usually, I managed to miss my brother...

My uncle kept all of his magic items in two locked suitcases. I remember obsessing about wanting to look in the suitcases, and trying to look in them on a number of occasions. It wasn't until many years later, when he passed away, that I finally had my chance. When he died, I said to my grandparents, if I was allowed, I would like two things of my uncle's. One was all of his magic things, the other was an old stuffed owl. Luckily, I managed to get both, and I finally had a chance to look through his magic suitcases.

Because I didn't feel I had any role models I could relate to as a child, I started looking elsewhere. I looked to my grandad as the type of adult I would like to be when I grew up; and I shared certain interests with my uncle - as he seemed to like puzzles and solving problems, and was a magician. My main role model during my primary years was Christopher Reeve as Superman. This has remained, even now as an adult. I remember reading an article about how many children like Superman when they are children, because of his superpowers and colourful costume. Apparently, most people grow out of seeing Superman as their favourite superhero as they grow up, though, because he is 'two-dimensional', and people gravitate towards superheroes like Batman who have emotional depth and complexity.

This definitely wasn't my experience. As an adult, I like Batman, and many other superheroes as characters, but I don't relate to them; they are just characters, and many of them have traits I can't relate to - or traits that would annoy me if I ever knew them. Many superheroes seem to be quite arrogant or too emotional. They seem to make their own lives very complicated by overthinking the wrong things. On the other hand, with Superman, I was able to relate to the character. Clark Kent was generally calm and humble. He knew he had special powers; he knew he could protect himself against attackers - like when he was young and in school and experiencing bullying - yet he learnt to restrain himself. He didn't feel he had anything to prove to them. As he grew up, his superpowers started to develop and his senses became heightened. He had to learn how to keep calm - how to manage the incoming stimuli and not let them overwhelm him. He had to learn to be able to focus his attention on one thing and ignore the rest.

This I could relate to. My hearing was overwhelmed by busy noises, my vision was overwhelmed by constant movement and complexity. There was so much to try to focus on and keep track of, and everything was uncomfortably bright. My body was full of constant sensations of irritation from my clothes, and my hair on my head, and trying to sit comfortably. I remember watching Superman when I was about seven or eight. I had probably seen it before, but I had to reach a certain mental maturity to understand Superman, and to make parallels with myself. I saw how Superman had to learn to focus on one thing and exclude everything else, I could understand that he had to learn to control his focus of attention if he was to prevent feeling overwhelmed. This is what I realised I also had to do.

One aspect of me that I saw in Superman was how he would anonymously save people, wouldn't take credit for it, and would carry on as Clark Kent - acting calm, passive and bumbling. He didn't try to take credit for what he had done; he was comfortable with people speculating and focusing on the Superman persona, while their focus wasn't on him as Clark Kent. I started developing this idea more from then on, through to who I am now as an adult. I wanted to be like Superman: calm and focused and in control of myself as a being. Someone who anonymously helps others and tries to keep all focus and attention off me as the agent of change; someone who knows what I can and can't do, but doesn't feel a need to prove that to anyone.

Many children love creating dens at home. I was no exception to this. I used to put sheets over my grandparents' dining room table, or arrange the dining room chairs with the seats facing outwards and lay sheets over the chairs. I don't know why other children make dens like this, but I know why I did. For me, it was somewhere calm and enclosed, where I could sit in a dark and safe environment. I rarely managed to make a den that was totally dark, but I could make it comfortably dark - like the light at dusk as the sun is setting. The light level would usually be reasonably even, which I also found comforting. I always liked dark and quiet areas. I would crawl under the bed, which was quite a squeeze, but being stuck tightly under the bed in the dark would feel comfortable. I would also sit in rooms in the dark.

I remember getting my first digital watch. I was probably about six or seven years old. The watch had a light on it behind the screen. The light didn't work very well for what it was designed. When it was turned on in the dark, it over-lit one side of the watch so you couldn't read that part of the time; it lit the middle of the watch about right to be able to read what the middle said; but it wasn't bright enough to light the far side of the watch. Obviously, people are very good at recognising patterns, so you could look at the part of the screen which was adequately lit and work out what the rest of the watch was likely to say - especially given you know roughly the time of day already. You couldn't really make out the seconds, or the first or last digit of the time, but you could make out the middle two digits. If the second digit was zero and it was night-time, logically, it must have been 10pm; if the second digit was one it must have been 11pm or 1am; and if the second digit was two, it could have been midnight or 2am. The third digit could narrow it down as to which ten-minute period it was, because you would see zero, one, two, three, four or five. You couldn't tell which minute it was unless you watched closely and saw the time change to a different number - in which case, the final digit must have just changed to a zero.

The main thing I remember about my watch - and each digital watch I had following that first watch, for some reason - I decided one day to look closely at the light. I began putting my left eye right up to the watch face and then squinting my eye to block out some of the light, so that I could see some detail. It was an unusual experience; I remember thinking it looked almost like a living system. I found it incredibly comforting to look at the light in the watch, and I remember it giving me a feeling - the whole time I was able to hold all of my attention on that light, I couldn't see anything else. It felt like I was floating in space, just outside of a solar system, watching planets orbiting a star surrounded by gas and dust. I even found the constant audible tone of the light relaxing and calming. When we moved from the house we were living in at the time I had that first watch, I remember it going missing, and I remember being upset about this. I kept playing in my mind with this belief that it went missing because I had hidden it under the carpet on the landing at the old address, for safe keeping. I don't know if I had, but I remember playing that thought in my mind over and over again - I believed that from as soon as we moved.

One thing which can be an issue, in my experience of Asperger's, is how my mind comes to certain conclusions. I often come up with a logical response to something which is, on reflection, probably not the best response to have. An example of this is when I was about ten years old. One of my brothers and I arrived home from school. No-one was home, so we let ourselves in, and then I went back outside to play with my skateboard. After spending time skateboarding down our garden path, which sloped down towards the house, then walking my skateboard back to the top of the path and skateboarding down again - and doing this repeatedly a number of times - I needed the toilet. I went to the front door and knocked for my brother to let me in. My brother didn't open the door, so I knocked again. I told him I wanted to come in because I needed the toilet. He appeared to think it was funny not to let me in. I'm sure many brothers would do the same and also think they are just having a laugh - but to me it wasn't fun, and it wasn't having a laugh. I couldn't understand any logical reason for his behaviour. I had told him I needed the toilet, and he knew I needed to come inside to go to the loo, yet he wasn't letting me in. From my perspective, I hadn't done anything horrible to him, so I couldn't work out why he would be doing something horrible to me.

Stood at the front door and trying to convince my brother to open up, I started thinking of what I should do. I needed the toilet and I knew I had to go very soon; I had to find a way of getting indoors. After a few minutes, I thought of a way of getting into the house. I told my brother that if he didn't open the door, I was going to smash through the door's window and open it myself. He didn't seem to believe me, so I raised my skateboard and swung it as hard as I could against the window. The window cracked when I hit it. I was about to strike it again, but breaking the window was enough to encourage him to open the door and let me in.

On reflection now, as an adult, I'm sure I could have come up with better solutions. My focus at the time was 'I need to get into the house', rather than 'I need the toilet', even though my reason for wanting to get into the house was to use the toilet, so my focus was on finding a logical solution to getting into the house. Had I been finding a logical solution for going to the toilet, I would have had many - much less destructive - options open to me. I lived in the countryside. I could have gone over the road into the fields and been out of sight and able to go to the loo, or I could have walked into the back garden and found somewhere out of sight to go in the back garden. None of this occurred to me at the time.

I think this is something that happens with many children with Asperger's: they find a logical way out of the situation, but are perhaps focusing on solving the wrong part of the problem. If they were able to step outside their current thinking, and gain a 'meta' position, they may get a broader focus about what is going on. These actions by me could be seen as aggressive, but I was just using the logical solution I had come up with to solve the problem, I hadn't lost control and become aggressive; I was being aggressive *because* it was the solution to gain control again.

I definitely don't advocate the use of aggression to gain control, and with all of my work over the years with victims of domestic abuse - partners, parents and children/teenagers - I think it is something which needs addressing if someone appears to want to control everything, and if someone uses aggression in its many forms to control situations. One thing I have had to learn is that, for healthy relationships, I have to not have control. There are things I don't want to control, because I don't particularly care about them - like where my wife is, who she is with, or what she is up to. None of that interests me. I only think about it if she is due to be somewhere and isn't there when I expect her to be. Then, depending on the situation, I eventually show concern, because I want to know she is safe and well.

But, that said, I can see how easy it would be for someone with Asperger's who wants to control their environment to develop an unhealthy level of control - perhaps over people in their life, rather than just their environment - and the control over their environment could easily also become unhealthy. If you are a parent of a child who seems to be displaying controlling behaviour, it is important to demonstrate comfort and support, and to acknowledge the child's difficulties and feelings whilst also maintaining that the boundaries and consequences are what they are. This can feel difficult at times, but it is very important.

It is also important to get help and support for your child. If they can learn to relax, and learn to handle uncertainty, they will learn to cope much better with life and with others as they grow up. I learnt to relax because I grew up in the country and had somewhere to go to relax, but I have never been very good with uncertainty, so some situations I will still feel uncomfortable in. Then, I will focus on behaviours which relax me and hope that the uncertainty ends. Other times, I will just escape the situation to escape the uncertainty. If I am able to, I will try to reframe the situation in some way to have some elements of certainty in the situation - enough for me to latch on to, to get through it. It is really helpful if these skills can be taught whilst the child is young, so that they can develop them as they grow up.

I have always had an issue with the toilet. As a child (and this persisted into my teenage years), I would wet and soil myself rather than ask to go to the toilet. I would hold out as long as I could, but asking was such a difficult thing to do. What if I asked to use the toilet and the person said no? What if I needed the toilet, went to go, and someone else was in there, and they were in there for a long time? I wouldn't be able to tell them to leave the toilet. Whenever I was out anywhere, I would try to hold needing the toilet until I got home. Even then, having a mum, stepdad and three brothers at home didn't guarantee the loo would be free to use. But at least if it was free, I didn't need to ask.

One day, mum took me and my brothers to someone's house. I can't remember whose house it was, but I remember they had children. I spent the duration of the stay at this family's house sat in their back garden with their kittens, just stroking the kittens and letting them climb on me. I needed the toilet, but couldn't figure out how to ask. I tried to hold in going to the toilet as long as I could. Unfortunately, I ended up wetting myself. I remember going back to the car when it was time to leave and being told off by my mum, which drew attention to the fact I had wet myself in front of the family - both the parents and children. I remember feeling embarrassed by this, yet helpless. I didn't feel there was anything I could have done differently. I couldn't have asked to go to the toilet because I didn't know for certain that they would say that I was allowed, or that it was free to use.

One of my coping strategies from a very young age was eating. I have never been a fussy or a picky eater. I will eat pretty much anything that is placed in front of me. In school, this made me very popular with the dinner staff. I would get given my food, sit and eat, then go up for seconds, and thirds - in fact, as many courses as I was allowed in the time I had. This may sound like I was a dream child. Many parents probably wish their children would eat whatever they are given, rather than say they don't like this or that. But on the inside, the story was quite different.

My relationship with food is an odd one. I have always told people how much I hate eating. From childhood, I have always thought that one day someone will invent a pill that can be taken in place of food. I don't get enjoyment from eating. I generally find food bland and tasteless. I am aware that different foods have flavours, but my only way to describe them is as tasteless. I have always wanted to eat strong flavours for this reason. I also find that, to feel like I get something from the food, I want a large quantity of it. I have always been a quantity-over-quality person. The thing is, when I am eating, I am usually getting angry with the process of eating. I remember, as a child, finding it arduous to eat food. It was always a chore. Eating is a challenge. About half the time I eat, I will end up biting the inside of my mouth or my tongue. I have always found that closing my eyes helps me to focus on eating safely. I was aware from a very young age that people often seemed to close their eyes as they put food in their mouth. I have always wondered whether this is a protective throwback from our past, when we may have been hunting and eating prey that could still be alive and which may harm us - in the same way sharks roll their eyes back in their heads to protect them when they strike their prey.

Eating is one of those things which seems paradoxical to me. I don't like eating, yet if I am going to eat, I have to eat a lot - and while I'm eating, I am usually getting angry with it. I'm glad when I finally finish eating, yet I decided to eat a lot. I would be finished quicker if I ate less…

I don't really get much taste from foods, but I like textures of foods. I remember in primary school, I liked semolina because of the texture. I could easily sit for hours placing spoonful after spoonful into my mouth - as long as it was lukewarm and not too hot or cold. Steak is another food of which I like the texture, and beef. I remember as a young child having a roast dinner at home. Following the roast dinner, there was some meat left over, so I had a big chunk of the meat. I took it to my bedroom with me and spent hours chewing, until I was ready to go to sleep. At that point, I placed the chewed meat on the windowsill so that I could continue to chew on it in the morning. I wasn't trying to eat the meat, as such, I was trying to make it last as long as I could as something to chew on.

My main reason for constant eating is because, while I am eating, I don't have to join in with anything. I realised if I sat in the dinner hall in primary school and ate my food, I would finish my firsts just before everyone else usually, and so would get seconds. Then everyone else would finish their firsts and wouldn't want seconds. So they would all go and play while I got to sit on my own and eat. Occasionally, a teacher or dinner person would come over and comment, praising me for my eating. I would look up and smile and carry on, but they wouldn't push me to go and play. I don't know if this would be different nowadays…

Back when I was a young child if you ate a lot of food, everyone praised you and told parents what a healthy appetite you had - meaning 'your child eats well'. When I used to visit my grandparents as a young child, they would say the same thing. They didn't mean I was eating healthy food, although most of what I ate was reasonably healthy because I would eat whatever I was given - so as long as my parents, grandparents and the school were serving healthy food, then that was the main food I ate. Nowadays, I wonder whether a child eating almost non-stop would lead to the parents being told the child is over-eating, or whether the 'healthy appetite' remains?

Eating got me out of a lot of interaction with others. I could have a mouthful of food which would get me out of talking with others; I could have a plateful of food which would get me out of having to join in things. I would do this at parties I had to attend, and family events. I remember attending a family BBQ. All the children went off to play, and all of the adults were interacting with each other. I pulled up a seat at one end of the tables of food, and I ate all that was in front of me, before moving the chair along and eating what was in front of me at the next table. I continued until I had worked my way to the end of the row of tables. By then, it was time to go. I think there have only been a couple of times in my life I can remember 'feeling full', and feeling like I needed to stop eating. Normally, I would just be shovelling food into my mouth until it is all gone. Even though I hate eating, I feel I am supposed to eat everything in front of me. So I do.

Through my primary years, I started becoming aware of who I am, of what I like and dislike, and of how I was different to other children. I also started to develop strategies and ways of fitting in and coping, and appearing normal.

# CHAPTER FOUR

## *Secondary Years*

My secondary school years - from eleven to sixteen - were a time of inner discovery and deeper understanding about myself. I had been interested in science before I started secondary school, but the term 'science' had never been mentioned in either of the primary schools I'd attended. It wasn't until I started secondary school that I had the opportunity to learn what science was, and to talk with others (mainly the teachers) about science.

I was already on the back foot right from my first day in secondary school. I was the only child from my primary school going to the secondary school I was starting. I remember my first day; I remember how large the school was and how daunting it was to see all of these children and have all the confusion. Everything seemed so chaotic. Most of the children seemed to know each other already - they were laughing and playing with each other and we were all being told where we had to go. There, we were introduced to our new form tutor who we had to follow to our classroom.

There was one child destined to be in my class who was also stood on his own quietly. He looked nervous and overwhelmed. He was dressed in scruffy clothes and looked dirty, which I remember at the time seemed unusual for a child on the first day of school. I slowly moved over to him. I didn't talk to him, and initially he didn't talk to me. We walked into our new class, and I sat at the same table as him.

Secondary school was such an overwhelming experience. I struggled with many aspects of being in such a large school; it was as if someone had created an environment designed to cause as much anxiety as possible. In primary school there were only a few teachers, and classes were small. In secondary school, classes were larger, the children were noisier, and you didn't just have one teacher to spend time with all day every day. You had many teachers, and had lessons in many different classrooms spread out over the large school grounds.

Every morning started in the same classroom with our form tutor for registration. Some mornings we had assembly, too. I used to dislike assembly - it was so crowded and I never knew what I was supposed to say or do, which just increased my anxiety. Following registration, I had to find my way to my first lesson. We had about five minutes to get there, and about five minutes between each class to get to the next lesson, unless there was a break time. Something about how my brain works makes this process very difficult. It sounds simple enough, for sure - the bell goes, you leave the class and walk to the next lesson - but, in reality, I seem to have a poor ability for remembering or recognising where I need to go. I wouldn't describe it as poor spatial awareness. I can do the spatial awareness puzzles where you are shown a picture of a shape and asked to choose which of the answers is the same shape, but from a different angle. I can usually get these fairly quickly. I can look at a map, orientate it in my mind, or just turn the map, and navigate well from maps - but I can't seem to work out where to go in the 'real world'.

This was an issue in a large school where I had to find my way from one class to another with a time limit. I think I always succeeded, but I remember finding it very stressful. It didn't matter how many times I walked a route, or how much I had been around the school; I would still struggle to find my way around. It used to cause me so much anxiety. When I was put on the spot, I would try to make any excuse to get out of the situation. If I was told to take something to another teacher or classroom, or if the room a lesson was normally in was changed, I would start to panic and have to focus on calming myself down. I didn't want people to see me panicking, in case they asked me if I was alright or tried to talk to me. At these times, I wanted the panic to calm down, I wanted to focus inwardly on breathing and relaxing - and not to have the additional stress of having to talk to someone.

The difficulty with school is that things are always changing; there are always new experiences just around the corner - whether it is having to join in different sports in physical education, or different events happening throughout the year, or just a change of teacher or class. I like structure. I like being told what to do, and how I am supposed to act. I like having structure that doesn't change. I am aware any new situation initially takes some getting used to, and it is normal for most people to feel uncomfortable in new situations - but some types of situations, I never seemed to get used to. I would rather go to school and have all my lessons in one class, or - at worst - have all the lessons in a few classrooms next to each other. In all the years I attended secondary school, I never got used to where to go to lessons, even though for some subjects I may attend a specific classroom three or four times a week.

When change occurred at school, I would struggle with my very black and white thinking about things. I was happy just not to do something if it made me uncomfortable, regardless of the consequences. In fact, I wouldn't even consider the consequences; I would just do what would make me feel most comfortable. I would fight this in situations where I felt I was supposed to do something for a good reason - in the same way that most people who are nervous about public speaking will still do it if they feel it is the right thing to do, but they may not go out of their way to do it, and are very unlikely to volunteer to speak in public.

The real question is: what is a good reason? What motivated me to keep control of myself and not just walk out of situations? I would be curious about answers others would give to this question. For me, it definitely wasn't like I felt obliged to do something, or that I was doing something because someone would be upset if I didn't. I didn't care what others thought of me; what made me decide whether to do something or not was how important I felt it was to me. For example, back when I was young, computers hadn't really come into schools. It was pre-Windows 95, so there were no clear operating systems, and each computer worked with different-sized disks. Over my years in school, I learnt a bit about computers, but it wasn't until Business Studies that we really had to use computers on a regular basis. I enjoyed some aspects of Business Studies, but didn't like having to use the computers. I was sure I would do something wrong that would break the one I was working on. I liked doing things with pen and paper. I liked doing business exercises. But for much of what I was learning, I couldn't see how it was going to be of benefit to me at that time.

I have always worked better by learning what I needed when I needed it, and when I decided to learn it. When I was approaching my GCSE exams, I told mum that I didn't want to take the Business Studies exam, and didn't want to do many of the other subjects I was learning. I wanted to just focus on English Language, Mathematics, and Science. I didn't see that Religious Education, Integrated Humanities, Business Studies, French and Physical Education were going to benefit me in any way. My focus at that time was on wanting to get the qualifications that employers wanted me to have. I was always told you needed good grades in English, Maths and Science.

I loved learning and really wanted to go to university. Specifically, I wanted to study a science subject in university, but again, the focus was always on needing good qualifications in English, Maths and Science. So, to me, these were the lessons I needed to focus on. I wasn't good at mental arithmetic. I could understand maths and could work things out - I just couldn't do it in my head. In one of my first maths lessons in secondary school, we had to do something with times tables, I said I didn't know my times tables, and asked if we could be taught them. The response I got was: "If you don't know them by now you never will. We don't teach that, you should have learnt that in primary school." It didn't seem to matter that I hadn't been taught times tables in primary school - not the way I see it done on television, anyway, with people learning to recite them so that they know them off the top of their head. We had been given the 100-square grid to see the patterns, and we were given plastic work cards with different maths problems on, which were really easy to complete. I always used either my fingers or paper to work out the answers, so I never learnt to do it any other way.

Once the teacher told me this I knew there was never any point asking teachers for help, because they would only teach what they were told to teach, and wouldn't listen if someone said they couldn't do something. They had a whole class to teach, and couldn't be teaching one person in the class one thing when everyone else in the class needed to be learning something else. This one experience stopped me ever asking questions in class again if I felt I needed help.

My black and white thinking often led to me making decisions like this. I now look back on them as I type, and I think about how stupid they were, yet I know I would make the same decision again if I was in the same situation - never mind how hard I would try not to do so.

When I was young, I was very good at running. I wasn't the fastest runner. I know people who were competitive and so would win races, but I could run an approximate six-minute mile over any distance I ran - from two-mile races, up to 26 miles (at this distance, my time had slowed to almost seven minutes per mile). My reason for running was because it was quicker than walking. I lived in the countryside, so if I wanted to get anywhere fast I ran there. Because I was good at running, I was entered into the school road running competition representing my group. I told the teacher I didn't want to run in the race. He told me he knew I was good at running so I was being entered. I explained that I had no interest in running around roads for no reason other than to beat the other children. I explained I wasn't happy to run just for the sake of running, and that if I was entered, I would walk. Despite making all this clear, I was entered, and I walked. I don't think people were happy with me; they would have done better to listen to me and enter someone competitive who would have run to try to win.

In all my reports from the years when I was in secondary school, there are certain things that crop up from almost every teacher across all the years. They all say: "Daniel needs to speak up and contribute in class more", and "Daniel needs to improve his concentration". From my reports, I come across as a very average child. The reports had four tick-boxes for each heading about how I was doing in each lesson. I was always hovering in the middle two boxes. Teachers I didn't get on with at all would often mark me in the lower middle or bottom box, and teachers with whom I got on better would usually tick the upper middle box. The exceptions were Science and Music, where I got on well with some of the teachers I had over the years; they gave me some ticks in the top box.

When I first started at secondary school, I found it so difficult that I asked my mum if there was a way I could be kept back a year. I was an August child who was due in September, so I was aware that - had I been born in September rather than August - I would be in the year below. My thinking at the time was that the extra year may have given me the time to 'grow up' and be better able to handle secondary school. Unfortunately, I didn't manage to convince anyone to hold me back a year. I didn't like or dislike school. As with everything else in my life, there are things I like and things I don't like. But I do feel that, if someone had noticed how anxious I was about certain things and how much I struggled with some things, I may have got help and I may have been placed in a smaller class.

I had never heard about special needs; I assume from the work I have done as an adult that the school probably had classes for children who needed additional support, and probably even provision for additional support for certain students in 'normal' classes - although, as a child, I never saw signs of this. I think I was largely overlooked in my class. There were probably about 30 children in the class, and unfortunately I seemed to share a class with a number of very disruptive students, whereas I was generally quiet. I wouldn't argue about things I thought weren't worth arguing about, I generally didn't like talking to people about things I wasn't interested in, so I wouldn't talk to other students, and wouldn't talk to teachers unless it was about something I wanted to talk about. This meant I didn't chat or 'mess around' in class. I didn't gossip. I generally kept myself to myself, regardless of what else was going on in the class.

Obviously - like most children - I did occasionally join in things if it interested me to do so. If I had no interest in what a teacher was saying and the child sat next to me was willing to talk about something I was more interested in, I would happily talk to that child. If the child next to me was being studious and was engaging in the class which I had no interest in, then I didn't mess around to try to get attention. I was more than comfortable occupying myself. I would focus on my own thoughts or just listen to music and doodle on folders or books. I used to have a Walkman in my pocket with in-ear headphones running up my school jumper and down my right sleeve into the palm of my hand. I worked out that teachers are more preoccupied with children towards the back of the class; frequently, the poorly-behaved children would sit back there - I assume - thinking that they could whisper to each other and misbehave without being noticed. But in reality, that is where teachers spend most of their time focusing.

I used to sit next to the overhead projector, with the projector on my left side. That way, I could copy what was on the projector rather than wasting my time listening to the teacher. I would be leaning on my right hand listening to music, and if the child sat next to me was also uninterested in what the teacher had to say, then I would have the left headphone running up their jumper into their left hand, and would let them copy what I was copying. This usually worked well, because I'm left-handed, and people sat next to me were always right-handed. I luckily never sat next to a left-handed person who wanted to listen to music with me.

For those younger people who are reading this, the Walkman I had in my pocket was a huge device that played cassette tapes. It was noisy to start and stop, as it wasn't like modern MP3 players, or even portable CD players. It had mechanical buttons which you had to press down, and they popped up noisily when the cassette tape stopped playing. If you wanted to 'skip' forward or backward through the audio you had to fast forward or rewind - you had to guess how far you needed to do that - and, as cassettes tapes are made of 'tape', it has to wind through the tape, which is also a noisy process. To listen to the other side of the tape (which may sound odd if you are very young, given that even CDs play everything on one side), you had to stop the Walkman playing, open it, take out the tape and put it back in with the opposite side facing towards the motorised spindles. So, in a class, you would have to figure out how to do all this quietly under the teacher's nose without drawing any attention to yourself.

Overhead projectors were large box-shaped devices with a very bright light in them, shining straight upwards and illuminating acetate transparent sheets, on to which the teacher would have written work. Above the light box was a mirror which could be angled at the screen at the front of the class. Teachers would normally have most of the clear sheet covered with a sheet of paper, and would pull the paper down little by little to reveal just the section they were teaching at that time, so they may say the topic we were covering in the lesson, and as they told us, they would slide the paper down to reveal the title which would be projected onto the screen.

Something I always found interesting was how the light didn't project what was on the acetate through the paper - the paper would show as totally dark on the screen - yet if you looked at the light box you could see what was on the acetate clearly through the paper. This meant you could copy what was written on the sheet if you looked at the light box, but you didn't know what was coming next if you were sat unable to see the top of the projector. This was also helpful for giving answers to questions the teacher would ask. Often they would reveal a question whilst keeping the answer covered. They would ask the class the question and ask what the answer was. I never voluntarily put my hand up to answer questions, but if I was singled out and hadn't been paying attention, I would have already read the answer, so I would just say what the answer was from this.

It was only when I went to secondary school that I had a Walkman. Prior to this, I could listen to cassette tapes or the radio at home on a hi-fi system we had, and at my grandparents' home I could also listen to records. I used to love the feel of records. I remember as a child liking the weight of them, the texture, and the way the light reflected off it. We were never allowed to touch the face of the record; we were always told to handle them with care and only touch the edges. This meant the records had no fingerprints on them - they were clean and dust-free. I loved the way the dark black would reflect light. They were also interesting to watch as they played. The record would just be a flat object with a continuous spiral groove running from the outside of the record towards the middle of the record. At the time, I didn't know how records worked, but it fascinated me that a small spike resting in the groove led to 'reading' a hidden message on the record which then 'spoke', or sung, that hidden message. There was something I found relaxing about watching a record spinning as it played.

When I got a Walkman, I was suddenly able to listen to music wherever I was. I wasn't that into music in the same way that my brothers and friends were. Most music sounded too chaotic, or had too much singing. I found many songs overwhelming to try to keep track of and follow. As a younger child, I had become interested in the music of Elvis Presley. Something about his music resonated with me. I preferred his slow ballads rather than faster songs like *Hound Dog* or *Blue Suede Shoes*. Slow songs are definitely more the pace of my mind. As an adult, I occasionally like faster songs, but even then I prefer specific faster songs - normally a song which somehow moves me, or makes me want to move, or matches what I am trying to do, like if I want to walk faster.

Normally I would like very specific songs and would listen to those songs repeatedly. One day, I made an accidental discovery. I had recorded some music from one tape to another, over the top of the music I had previously recorded. Unbeknown to me at the time, the tape recorder was set to record in mono rather than stereo. I didn't realise this until I was listening to the tape through my Walkman, when I noticed that the original recording could be heard playing through one earpiece, and the new recording had only recorded over half of the previous recording and could be heard playing through the other earpiece.

This interested me. Suddenly I had a way to listen to different music without having to change the tape. I recorded a Michael Jackson album onto a tape in stereo, and then recorded a Queen album over the top of the Michael Jackson recording in mono. This allowed me to listen to both albums at the same time.

Having said about not liking chaotic music and songs with too much singing, this may sound like I was creating my own problem - but to be aware of both in such a way as you could enjoy them... You had to let go and not be focusing on either. You had to learn to hover in the middle of the experience. When you are doing this, you also start to shut out the rest of the world. Not because you are trying to shut out the world, but because you are getting into a state of mind where you aren't specifically focusing on anything; you are just being mindful of the ongoing experience, almost allowing both ears to hear what is being played into that ear and enjoy its own music independently of the other. Focusing on either one would almost cancel out the other one. I have never been very good at narrowing my focus in that way by choice - I am much better at detaching from things than I am at attaching to things. This has always been a problem when people talk to me in noisy or chaotic environments. I struggle to be able to cancel out everything but the person talking to me. I am much better at being passive and zoning out and entering a more relaxed state where I don't feel so overwhelmed; I tend to just let someone talk as I listen, and often, I find I have picked more up this way. However, my experience is that people then think I am not listening, or they get frustrated with me; yet, when I try to focus on the person talking to me and keep saying I can't hear or understand them, they also get frustrated with me.

Normally, as a teenager, I would start out with a couple of albums which I would listen to repeatedly for a few weeks (two albums at a time), but eventually I would find I only really liked one song. I would then record just this song repeatedly onto both sides of the tape. If there were a few songs I liked, I would carefully record a song, turn the tape over and record the same song. Then, I would turn the tape over, play the song I'd just recorded, and once it finished, I'd record the second song, turn the tape over and record the second song again. Then, of course, I'd turn the tape over, play the song, and once it finished, I'd record the third song, then turn the tape over and record the third song. I'd keep repeating this until I filled the tape on both sides with each song in the same location on both sides of the tape. When I was about 14, I got a Walkman that had a reverse switch. This meant I could stop the tape, flick the switch, then start the tape and the Walkman would be playing the opposite side of the tape. I wouldn't have to remove the tape from the Walkman and physically turn it over. I was able to listen to a song, stop the tape, flick the switch, start the tape and listen to the same song now playing on the other side of the tape.

## The magic of learning

Something secondary school taught me was how much I actually enjoyed learning. I already knew I liked learning, but the learning opportunities I had in primary school were limited, and I rarely felt stimulated. Secondary school, meanwhile, taught me science; it went more into history than primary school did, and I enjoyed learning about geography and religious beliefs, too. There was so much more to learn. What I didn't like was the idea of having to learn just to do a test, or to learn and then do a project in some way, so as to show what I had learnt. Ideally, I would have just attended the lessons to learn from, and had the opportunity to ask teachers questions about the material I was learning. I didn't want to waste my time doing homework or coursework or tests; I just wanted to be taught.

Occasionally, teachers would set homework in a way that allowed me to do things my way. If the work I had to do was to answer questions I didn't care about, I was unlikely to do it - it wouldn't interest me enough to waste my time on it. Some of my favourite projects included a World War Two history project. I can't remember what we were told to do specifically, but I know the project was set in a way that essentially guided us towards writing an essay. Because of the wording, though, I realised I could do the project much more easily. I had no motivation to sit and write about World War Two, so when I was at my grandparents' house - and some of my older relatives were there - I asked if I could tape record interviews with them about their different experiences during the war. I did this over the space of about 40 minutes, and submitted the tape as my coursework with a brief covering page explaining what I had done and what was on the tape. I got an 'A' for my work, yet all I was doing was trying to make the task as simple and interesting as possible for myself. I was genuinely interested in what life was like during the war; I felt books showed pictures, but I wanted to know what it was like for real people, whom I knew.

I found many teachers in my secondary school didn't understand me and weren't helpful at all. They wouldn't pick up that I needed help, but there was one teacher who stands out to me as someone who helped me immensely, and without some advice from her, I would have done far worse in school and I wouldn't have written the books I have written - including this one you're reading now.

During my first year in secondary school, we had a science project, where we had to build a bridge out of cotton and spaghetti, and then see how much weight our different bridges could hold. I built a suspension bridge. What we were told to do was to build a bridge out of the materials, and then to write what we did. In the next lesson, we would test to see which bridge could hold the most weight. So I built the bridge and wrote: "I built a bridge out of cotton and spaghetti." The teacher asked me if my parents had made the bridge. I told her that they wouldn't have been clever enough to know to make a suspension bridge. She didn't believe I'd made the bridge because I had shown no evidence that I knew how to build one - or knowledge of why I would build the particular bridge I built. All I had written was that I had built a bridge out of cotton and spaghetti. I told the teacher why I had built the bridge. I explained about the strength of suspension bridges given the materials we had, and about how the cotton was able to take a lot of the weight through the structure, so that the bridge could hold more weight than a simple beam bridge could. Dry spaghetti, placed horizontally across two upright spaghetti pillars was likely only to hold a certain amount of weight before it cracked, as dry spaghetti isn't very flexible. Cotton wrapped under the spaghetti, from cotton above the spaghetti, over to the other side and up to cotton above the other side and then wrapped back down under the spaghetti again and back to the other side, however, would allow the cotton to support the weight along the length and width of the bridge.

The teacher replied that what I had said was what she wanted written down, because it showed I had evaluated the task, and understood what I had to achieve. I had evaluated different bridge structures in relation to the task and given my reasons for developing the specific bridge, and then I had built it. I said the question didn't make that clear, it asked me what I did - not how or why I did it. She said that there would be lots of times in school when questions were written like that; normally they would want you to answer more fully. She said I should write down what I would say to someone if they asked me what I did and why, and just put everything down on paper. She told me I could always learn how to edit and make changes to the work - but if it wasn't written down in the first place, I wouldn't be showing evidence of what I knew. She said sometimes I may be told I had written too much, or in too much detail, or with some unnecessary information, but I could learn from being told that as I went through school.

This advice was huge to me. It stood out straight away and has remained prominent in my mind ever since that day in 1989. I still naturally find myself being blunt and giving curt answers to things as my more default setting. That is, unless I want to share lots of information about a subject I enjoy, because I think someone else should also know about it. Often, that teacher's words come into my mind when I catch myself doing that, and I think about whether I have missed out information that the reader, or listener, would probably have wanted to know.

I've already shared about an unhelpful maths teacher who just dismissed my comments about needing help. Most other teachers weren't that dismissive - they just didn't seem to notice I needed help. I don't know if this was more to do with a lack of understanding about problems children faced back then. Nowadays, I go into many schools, both primary and secondary. All of the teachers I speak to know about autism spectrum disorder. They speak to mental health practitioners for advice about children, and whether the mental health practitioners think the child they are talking about has Asperger's. Whether a child has a condition or not, they look at how to meet the child's needs and whether there can be additional funding they can use to help support that child. Unfortunately, funding is usually only available when a child has a diagnosis, yet I know many teachers who would like to be able to offer support to children who perhaps don't have a diagnosis. Sometimes, teachers can find ways around this and get the support. But I don't remember any of this from when I was in school. Every school report of mine says the same thing from each different teacher. Allegedly, the reports were read by my form tutor and the head of the section we were in; then, the Head or Deputy Head of the school signed each report and gave a comment about the student's progress. So, reading my reports it looks like more senior staff had read them, but if they truly had been read before being signed, these more senior staff seemed to miss the patterns that were there for all to see - where all the different teachers had said the same thing, every year.

It is this lack of awareness that I think let me down in secondary school, where I may have had extra help. I know Asperger's wasn't used as a diagnostic term until 1992, and didn't make it into the Diagnostic and Statistical Medical Manual (DSM-IV) until 1994 - as I was leaving secondary school in 1995, it was just coming into use as a term, and probably wasn't being taught widely to teachers until a couple of years later. I hadn't heard about autism until 1998, when I was working in mental health care homes, and hadn't heard about Asperger's until 2004, while working with children in care homes. I did try to tell teachers that I couldn't do some things, and couldn't understand some things, but I would just get told to do them anyway. My school reports for each lesson say I must try harder to concentrate in class, I must do my homework, I must speed up my writing and put effort into writing more, and I must contribute more in class.

When I left school with GCSEs, I had BB for Science, C for English Language, and C for Mathematics. I had a couple of Ds, and all my other grades were Fs. Yet people have always told me I am intelligent. I have always been surprised at how well children do nowadays. Many families I have worked with have children who barely attend school and yet leave with multiple A grades, often A*s, and yet I only managed a couple of Bs and Cs from all my lessons. I have always believed I was capable of achieving more; I just didn't seem to fit with exactly how school was done. I couldn't write quickly enough to finish exams; I wouldn't give all the information needed in essays because I wouldn't understand or know exactly what I was supposed to write; and I seemed totally incapable of doing things for which I couldn't understand a logical reason. I definitely would have benefited from a skilled, trained teacher who would work one-to-one with me, and from different settings for things like exams.

Classes always had too many children in them. I felt most comfortable if I was in a small group of no more than five or six children, all of whom I got on with. If there were more than that - or if there were children who bullied me - I would close down from the group. I think this can be a problem nowadays. Often, children who need additional support due to issues like being on the autistic spectrum get placed in the same group as children who misbehave, or are disruptive, or bully other children.

When I started attending secondary school, I was still living in Warningcamp and had to catch a school bus to Littlehampton. The bus was the same bus I'd had to catch to my primary school in Arundel. It picked up children from Warningcamp and the surrounding area, before heading into Arundel to drop children off at the two primary schools, then it travelled on to Littlehampton to the secondary school. Within a few weeks of starting the school, I found out that another child in my class also came from the Warningcamp area; this gave me someone to travel to and from school with.

Generally, I didn't have many friends. I have never been good at making and keeping friends, partly because I have no interest in making and keeping friends. My friends are very situational. It doesn't mean I don't 'like' the people I have been friends with, or that I don't see those people as being friends; even now as an adult, I just think about friendship in a different way to how other people talk about friendship. When I was friends with the person who lived near me, I used to visit his home most evenings after school. We used to build go-karts and tree camps, death slides and swings, and would occasionally go camping in fields. If it wasn't the weather for doing those sorts of things, my friend had a Nintendo Entertainment System (NES) the first Nintendo games console. We would play *Duck Hunt*, *Mario*, or *Track and Field*.

Once we moved to Littlehampton, mum felt we would then be closer to school and we would be able to attend activities easier - most clubs and activities took place in Littlehampton, whereas almost nothing took place in Warningcamp, and very little took place in Arundel. Because of this, I stopped spending time with the friend from near where I lived. I even stopped spending time with him in school. I met a new boy, who remained my main friend through most of the years I was in secondary school. He seemed to understand me better than most other children. He had a pool table in a building in his back garden, and he also had pool lessons. This was how I first learnt what pool was, and I very quickly fell in love with the game and started attending coaching sessions. Most of the other children I spent time with at this time were friends of my friend. I got on with most of them alright, but I only engaged with them because that is what 'we' were doing at that time. If my friend wanted to join in activities with them, then I joined in as well.

Towards the end of my time in secondary school, I moved on to my third set of friends. Again, I latched on to one friend. He had a Super Nintendo (SNES), which was the Nintendo console that came after the NES. The good thing, at least back when I was a child, is that children who played computer games were often children who didn't mix much with other children. Nowadays, it is different - playing computer games is more common among people. The games I would play most weren't multiplayer games; they would allow me to sit quietly with my friend watching him play, and then maybe have a go after him, playing on my own. I generally didn't like multiplayer or competitive games, which is the same now. The only game I think I really have enjoyed playing with others was as a young adult playing *Golden Eye* on the Nintendo 64 (N64).

This third set of friends enjoyed going to West Beach in Littlehampton to play manhunt. Manhunt has always been a favourite game, because it involves hiding, sneaking, practicing and developing skills - whether they be tracking, finding and catching people, or hiding, sneaking and avoiding capture. We used to also build camps on the beach, and would often play at night. Sometimes I would convince my friends to travel to Warningcamp with me to play games like manhunt in the woods.

I also attended a local youth club a couple of times per week with these friends. At the youth club, there were always children I wanted to avoid, because they would want to pick on me, and I preferred not being picked on. But the youth club did a wide range of activities I enjoyed. They had a Sega Megadrive which was often in use and difficult to get a go on - but I didn't own one, so would enjoy playing it when opportunities arose. They also did trampolining. I liked the feeling of weightlessness between bounces and would try to jump as high as I could, and hold onto that feeling for as long as possible. They did rifle shooting, where we got to shoot targets, or McDonald's Happy Meal figures lined up at the end of a hall. They also had an indoor basketball court. I wasn't very good at basketball as a game. I struggled with so much going on, and trying to keep track of people and the ball, but I loved the weight, smell and feel of a basketball, and the feel of it when it was thrown, and the noise it made as I bounced it. My favourite part of the noise was the silence between the sound of the ball hitting the ground, and the sound of the ball as it reached my hands again. I also enjoyed throwing the ball into the hoop. I could happily stand on the same spot for hours on end just throwing it in. One thing I always wanted to do was to slam-dunk the basketball. I was a short child, but I learnt that you can practice jumping higher by crouching all the way down to the floor, then pushing all the way up and jumping off the ground, then lowering back down again and repeating this. I practiced many hours a day for months until, eventually, I could stand below a basketball hoop and jump off the ground and just about reach the rim.

I was very good at practicing things for hours at a time - day after day if I wanted to learn it badly. I practiced holding a playing card, the wrong chosen card, and then flicking it and having the card in my hand now being the correct card. I practiced in front of a mirror, trying to move different facial muscles because I wanted to be able to show different facial expressions realistically, following learning about the differences between a 'real' smile and a 'fake' smile. I wanted my smiles to appear more real. I went through a stage where I was fascinated with ventriloquism. I loved how impressive it was that a ventriloquist could talk so fluently and 'normally' without moving the lips, so I would stand in front of a mirror for hours talking with my mouth closed. Likewise, when I started learning to play pool, I practiced for about thirty hours per week.

As soon as I was interested in something, I would become obsessed with it, and would assume that if I was obsessed with it, then everyone else must be as well. It is weird to think that people don't love what I love as much as me, but I keep being told that they don't. I would want to know every detail about the subject. I would want every book I could get about it. I would want to have everything connected to that subject. It would also become my main focus of attention and conversation. I never seemed to stop being interested in something, but over time, circumstances would make certain interests less intense, or I just reached a point where there didn't seem to be as much new information to learn. I kept a look out for anything new, but didn't spend all of my time focusing on that one thing. Even now, I also occasionally discover something new that interests me more. So I will continue to be interested in the other subjects, but prefer to focus on the subject that interests me most.

When I left school, it didn't cross my mind to keep in touch with friends that I had in school. I moved forward with my life, without giving any thought to those I knew. When I have seen those friends since school, I still treat them as friends, and they treat me as a friend, and the conversation normally ends with them saying we should meet up sometime - or a similar comment - and me agreeing. Then nothing happens; we just carry on in our separate ways.

Socially, I never really knew how I was supposed to behave in school. I didn't know or think about how I didn't know how to behave socially. I behaved in my own way, thinking that it was normal. Occasionally, other children would try to bully me, but many ways in which they would try to bully didn't register with me. I didn't really understand name-calling, other than it would annoy me that they were incorrect in what they were saying. If they tried to be funny, I often wouldn't understand them; if they acted angrily, I didn't get intimidated, because I didn't understand why I should be scared - they would just be saying words, they weren't doing anything to be scared of. If they became violent towards me and perhaps pushed me over, I didn't understand how I was supposed to react; I would just stand up and walk away. I didn't get scared by someone attacking me. I obviously didn't want to be hurt, so I would avoid situations where I thought someone may hurt me, but if someone was attacking me, I couldn't avoid it. All I could do was wait for them to finish what they were doing so that I could carry on with my day.

I remember once being attacked by a bully; they had some friends around them, who were encouraging them to attack me. I don't think they needed the extra encouragement, though - they had decided already that they were going to attack me. The bully pushed me over on the playing field. I stood up and carried on walking. I didn't say anything, because I didn't have anything to say. They pushed me over a few more times, and each time I just stood up and carried on walking. After a while, the bully said they could "deck me" if they wanted, before turning to the others and saying something like "let's go and do something else". I think they got bored of getting no reaction. Bullies usually want to bully someone they are confident they will be able to beat up; but they do still want to show their power or status, and want the person they are bullying either to be scared and cower, or to try to fight. By giving no reaction - not responding with fear or anger - I was a boring target.

I wasn't always passive, but it depended on the situation. I was never angry or fearful in situations like this, unless it was needed, because I knew what I was doing. I have always got anxious and blunt in situations where I feel like I am drowning in uncertainty, but if someone pushed me over, I knew I was going to just walk away. I had no interest in what they were doing so I wouldn't stay, but likewise I wasn't going to run unless I felt I was going to get hurt and running was the best available option. If I was very likely to get hurt and running wasn't an available option, then I would do whatever I had to do to give myself the best chance of getting out of the situation as safely as possible. Because I knew this was how I would react, I didn't have a reason to be fearful or angry unless it was needed to help me do what I had to do to maintain my safety.

In one situation, a child much larger than me who often bullied other children stole a chocolate bar from me whilst I was walking home. I was a much faster runner than he was, so I easily caught up with him. I calmly got him pinned to the ground where I caught up with him, which happened to be in the middle of the road on the A259 - quite a busy road through Littlehampton. I calmly and bluntly told him I wanted my Dairy Milk back. He was telling me I was crazy, as cars were driving around us and beeping at us. I wasn't focused at all on the cars; I was focused on the fact that he had taken my chocolate bar and I wanted it back. It belonged to me, and I was about to eat it on the way home. It didn't take long for him to return it. I had no concern for whether I could get run over or injured. It was solely a matter of principle.

I always tell myself I am never rude with people - I am just open and honest - but I do know a girl in school who repeatedly asked me out. I kept saying no to her, and eventually she asked me why. I told her she was ugly. I am aware now that she was probably upset because of this, yet to me this was just my opinion, and it was the honest answer to her question. My wife often tells me that the way I am when I'm open and honest and blunt about things comes across as rude, even if, in my head, I am not meaning to be rude. To me, if they decide to take what I have said as rude, then that is their choice; they are giving what I have said that meaning. I was comfortable being honest with teachers if they asked me a question, I never shouted at teachers - or anyone else, as far as I am aware. I think I have only shouted when I have been getting people's attention, but never aggressively, and I had no problem being honest with other students.

I have always had an issue with black and white thinking. I didn't know that phrase when I was a child, and I don't think I was aware that I had black and white thinking. Everything would be all or nothing. If anything changed, that was the point at which I would stop and completely give up. I have already mentioned a road running race, and refusing to run it at all. A couple of years later, I was in a race along the seafront at Littlehampton. We were told what the route was - straight along the seafront from the start line, to a specific location where we would turn around and run back again, crossing the start line from the opposite direction. I started fine; I ran to the checkpoint and started heading back the way we'd come. When I was about half a mile or less from the finish line, there was a marshal stood at a location where the road which runs along the side of the seafront turns inland. He said that the route had been altered, so we had to run down this road, then turn off into a road which turns left back parallel to the seafront. Then, we should take the turning along the side of the River Arun, before turning left again to cross the start/finish line in the same direction as we'd originally crossed it. I immediately stopped running. As soon as I was told that the route had changed, I had no interest in completing the race, so I just walked back to the finish line.

As far as I was concerned, I was supposed to do one thing, and I was doing that thing. I hadn't agreed to do something else, so I wasn't going to do it. As well as black and white thinking I can be stubborn even if I am the one who will suffer through my own stubbornness. These are traits I have always tried, and failed, to address throughout my life. The areas where my behaviour becomes most extreme socially are where something is about to be very uncomfortable for me. I don't like being touched. I am better able to handle it nowadays, but I definitely wasn't good at being touched when I was younger. I hated feeling trapped by people. So I was comfortable climbing into the trunk of an old tree, or squeezing my body down a small hole in the ground, or being wrapped tightly in blankets in a bed, but if children grabbed me to give me the bumps, or jumped on me while I was on the ground - then as soon as I felt I couldn't get out effortlessly, I would do whatever I had to do to get free. It was of no interest to me whether the people holding me got hurt or not - they chose their behaviours. So if their choice of behaviour led to them getting hurt - well - that was their decision. I always got free when children tried to bundle me or give me the bumps. I didn't care whether these children were my friends or not; I would say I didn't want something to happen and, if it did, I would do whatever I had to to end the situation.

Many stories I have heard from parents with children with ASD describe this happening to their children. I can hear the story and notice that the child didn't do anything wrong as far as they were concerned. They weren't trying to be aggressive or horrible, or even violent; they were just trying to escape a situation that made them feel uncomfortable; and they were willing to do whatever they had to in that situation to make sure they felt comfortable. Often, other adults - both professionals and parents - focus on the behaviour and the meaning *they* give to someone doing that kind of behaviour, rather than focusing on the meaning *the child* gives to the behaviour. Unfortunately many children don't know why they do what they do. As a teenager, if someone asked me why I behaved in that way, I don't think I would have known how to answer them. Most adults would probably phrase the questions to me as if I had done something wrong, which from my perspective wouldn't be correct. I would probably be confused, wondering what they'd meant - like in primary school when I was confused about the implication that I had been the cause of the fight in the playground.

I think it is important to talk to children with ASD about what they did, and explore what they can do differently next time, but not necessarily to place your own interpretations and judgements on their actions. The child may not be able to understand at that specific point in their life, so insight being given to the child isn't necessarily the best response; but, as a parent or professional, that insight can be helpful to you to understand the child better, and to understand how they may behave in the future, or even to develop ideas which can help the child find ways of managing situations differently. As an adult, I am the same person I was as a child. I don't feel any different, and I know if friends went to grab me to give me bumps because it was my birthday, I would do whatever I had to do to prevent that - even if it meant seriously hurting my friends. I wouldn't give it a second thought in that moment; my only thoughts would be on making sure I remained safe and comfortable. But what I do now - which I never would have thought to do as a child - is to make sure I am open about myself and make sure friends know this about me. Then, if they went to grab me, I would warn them that I didn't want to be grabbed, to give them a chance to change their minds. I used to tell people in school I didn't want them to do things like this, but in school, children don't listen and they try to do it anyway. If they decided to continue with their behaviours, then, as far as I was concerned, they were making that decision in the knowledge that I would get as aggressive as I needed to be to make myself comfortable. Luckily, no-one since my school days has tried to give me the bumps or bundle me, although it has occasionally been talked about by friends - at that point, I have made it clear it would be a bad idea!

Sometimes, having black and white thinking would lead to me making odd decisions. I remember being thirsty one day. I wanted something to drink. There wasn't anywhere to get free drinking water, and break time had ended. Someone I knew had a can of Lucozade Sport. I asked if I could have some. He said I could, if I paid him £5. So that is what I did. I didn't care how much the drink cost, I would have agreed to any price to get the drink, because I wanted it, and it was important to me in that moment to have a drink.

I think I used to drive many friends away as a teenager, because I would talk endlessly about my interests. I wouldn't talk about others' interests unless it was a shared one. I couldn't understand why anyone would want to talk about something I wasn't interested in. I would gravitate towards people who shared the same interests; I would talk to my uncle about magic at any chance I got, for instance. I would talk to my science teachers about science, and would want to stay after the lesson ended to be able to talk about what I was interested in about science - which usually wasn't the same thing that we were being taught in the lessons. In fact, I often wanted to talk to teachers more than my friends; to me, they were the ones who were supposed to be interested and knowledgeable in those subjects. I would often be late meeting up with friends at break and lunchtime, because I would be trying to talk to the teacher if my last class happened to be a subject I was interested in.

Science always fascinated me. I wanted to know everything; I wanted to fill my head with all the knowledge I could. Science was a subject about understanding everything. I started buying science magazines, including the first ever issue of *Focus* (now *BBC Focus*), of which I now have every single copy since it first came out. I started reading many different science magazines, and my grandparents subscribed to weekly children's science titles for me. I loved reading them, but quickly found science articles had more depth in magazines like *New Scientist* and *Scientific American* - both of which I have collected since I was in school. Science seemed to be all about problem-solving, and there was always something unknown to learn... It was such a broad topic. There is nothing more exciting than the first time you cut an onion and put it under a microscope and see individual cells, and the different parts of the cell. And then, at night, looking up at Saturn through a telescope, seeing the rings and moons and becoming absorbed in what you can see; the slight wobbling seems to almost draw you in more. It looks like it is all slowly moving as if you are in space, drifting and floating quietly towards the planet. Science opened up questions and possibilities, and stimulated my mind to think about different inventions and ideas.

As an adult who has worked with school teachers a lot in my professional work, I can see how this could have been most annoying for the teachers. They were probably looking forward to the break as much as the children! They probably had phone calls to make, and other jobs to do that I was keeping them from - but as a teenager, none of that crossed my mind. I will happily forgo meals to talk about my interests. I assumed teachers loved the subjects they were teaching. I never thought people became teachers because they wanted to teach; I thought it would be because they wanted to talk about that subject all day every day. So, as my teenage self, I would want a teacher to talk to me all break time on the subject I asked them about.

Teachers were definitely more polite than other children. Friends would eventually tell me to stop talking about things so much, whereas teachers would listen and, looking back on the memories, I suspect they were just politely waiting for a moment to say they would have loved to be able to keep talking but they had to be somewhere. As a teenager, I was never very good at noticing when people were bored or losing interest in what I was saying.

One difficulty with being interested in subjects like science was that I would give answers that were correct, but I would be told they are wrong. During a mock science exam, there was a question asking what gravity was. I answered that it was the warping of space/time - I was told this was incorrect. I showed the science teacher one of my science books where it talked about gravity in this way, and she responded that the answer I gave would be correct if I were doing a higher-level qualification, but the GCSE answer was "the attraction of two bodies towards each other". Another difficulty was that teachers would say things they didn't necessarily expect students to follow through with. A maths teacher said - in the last maths lesson before half term - that he would give £500 to anyone who could write down the twelve perfect numbers. He then explained to us what perfect numbers were and how to work them out, and told us the first few perfect numbers. The numbers get very large very quickly, so I used long multiplication and worked out all twelve perfect numbers - only I also found that there was a 13$^{th}$ number. but the twelfth number was so big I decided to stop where I had reached. When I went back in to school, I told the teacher I had found a 13$^{th}$ number but didn't work it all out. He told me he wouldn't give me £500, as I didn't work out 'all' the perfect numbers once I'd found there were more. I was very annoyed about this. My mum was also annoyed, as I had spent hours on this and had achieved what he had asked. My mum challenged him, but he still refused to pay out.

I used to have really messy handwriting. It is still often very messy and sometimes even too messy for me to understand what I have written. Being left-handed, I would smudge my work as I wrote because my hand would follow the writing. In primary school, my work often had comments on it about the fact that I was using my left hand to write. By secondary school, people didn't seem bothered that I was left-handed, but it does have its challenges - and no-one teaches you how to do things left-handed. I learnt that I wrote neater if I tilted my paper sideways so that I was writing downwards instead of across. This stopped my hand from following my work and smudging what I had just written. Some teachers would regularly criticise my handwriting, so I was always trying out different styles of handwriting that I saw other children doing, and tried to replicate neat handwriting styles, whether they were by other students, or I'd seen them in books. Some teachers would tell me to 'write properly' and straighten up my paper, but this was exactly what led to my writing being more messy and smudged.

I tried to learn calligraphy outside of school. I thought calligraphy looked nice and may have also helped me to learn to write neater. Turns out that I encountered an issue straight away. Calligraphy requires a pen with a wide nib which is slightly angled; this angle is in the wrong place for left-handed people, so you just end up scratching away at the paper. My nan purchased me a left-handed calligraphy pen to use, which was much easier. I liked doing calligraphy, but it wasn't very practical for school, so I only went through a short phase of doing all my school work in calligraphy writing. I tried writing with the letters slanting left, and with the letters slanting right; I found that slanting the letters left helped my hand stay out of the way more. I also tried bubble writing, which is what most other children seemed to do. I didn't like this, it looked too chaotic to me. Teachers criticised my writing, but I actually found the pattern of my writing relaxing, I liked the proportion of white space on the page to text, and the placing of where that white space was. I liked angles of the different letters, or just the overall look of the text as a whole. It wasn't always readable, but I liked how it looked.

Some teachers complained so much that I started being awkward with my writing in their lessons. I would sometimes write really small, I was able to fit about 130 words on a single line. I liked doing this because I would become absorbed in focusing on writing each letter so small; it would feel pleasurable in that state where I was focusing and writing like that. Other times, I would write everything backwards - mirror writing - and sometimes I would write with both hands at the same time, with one hand writing backwards and one writing forwards. My attitude was that I was asked to write a piece of work, and I wrote it. If the teacher couldn't read it, that wasn't my problem, I did what I was asked to do. This didn't always go down well with teachers, but at least when they now complained about my writing and not being able to read it, I felt they at least had something to complain about.

Dating was another issue in school. I generally had very little interest in people in school for any reason, whether as friends or girlfriends. I was far more interested in subjects than people. Children went out with each other in primary school, but I didn't have any interest in doing this, and for the first few years into secondary school I continued having no interest in going out with anyone. Then, one year, something odd happened. It turns out that for some reason people don't like asking other people out - they would prefer someone else to do it - so I asked out a girl for one of my friends. She said no. I asked her out for another one of my friends. She said no. Then another friend. Again, she said no. Then, I thought to myself: actually I quite like her... Why don't I ask her if she will go out with me? I couldn't understand why others wouldn't ask people out themselves - all you have to do is walk up to someone, ask them out, they give an answer, and...

It was this bit I needed to plan for. When asking her out for everyone else, it was easy. I'd walk up to her, I'd say, "So and so would like to go out with you," and she'd then say yes or no, at which point I'd walk back to my friends and tell them the answer. This was a clear structure I could follow and understand. If I asked her out for myself, and she said no, what would I do? Just say "okay" and walk away? Where did I need to go to justify just walking away? Should I stay and continue to talk with her? What would we talk about?

Likewise, if she said yes, what was I supposed to do? I would then be suddenly going out with this person - was I supposed to act or behave in a specific way?

In the end, I thought of a solution. I decided to ask her out just before the bell went at the end of the lunch break. That way, if she said yes, I had a planned action - the bell would go so I would quickly agree where to meet up next, and then leave. If she said no, the bell would go, I would say okay, and then I'd have to go because the bell had sounded.

I waited until the bell was about to ring, went over to the girl and asked her out. She said yes. Then the bell went. The odd thing was, all of a sudden, I wanted to stay. I had planned, as I always do, exactly how things should go and how I should react, and yet in the moment, I didn't want to react as I'd planned. It wasn't a long relationship - I think I was only superficially in it. I wanted to have the relationship and wanted to do everything right, but I was still following programmes I was creating in my mind based on stereotypes of what I thought I was supposed to do in that situation. I was kind, caring, supportive. I put her first. But I was also cold, not understanding the emotional and physical components of the relationship, or how important these bits are to others just because they weren't to me.

I remember the relationship ending after a few weeks. Nothing bad had happened - I mean, we hadn't argued or fallen out - but I could easily completely forget about the other person. I would be somewhere with them and become occupied in my own interests and pay no attention to them at all. We were at the local youth club when a teen approached me around the side of the club, pinned me to the wall aggressively, and told me she was now his girlfriend - I was to keep away from her or else he would 'sort me out'. I remember all I could muster in response: "Okay." Then I moved on and didn't think anything of it and never saw her again. I didn't think to find her and ask her about the relationship, about her feelings, and about what she wanted. I just accepted what I was told and moved on unquestioningly.

Following that relationship, I remember going through a stage where a number of different girls seemed to want to go out with me from the year below mine. I briefly went out with a few of them, but each relationship only lasted a day or two. I had no real interest in them. I don't think I was the boyfriend they hoped I would be. I don't think I showed the level of affection they would have liked, and I had very little interest in conversing with them. I remember some good times - like lying under the stars with a girl and just gazing up at the sky, and going to Warningcamp to go on a swing myself and a friend had built years earlier.

Eventually, I ended up in a couple of relationships with people from my own year in school. The first of these ended with us deciding we weren't suited for each other; the second time, the girl was too clingy for me. One day, I told her I didn't want to see her that day. The fair was on and I wanted to go to the fair. I met some friends there to go on the rides, and the girl turned up. I told her I was there with my friends and carried on going on different rides.

What I didn't know at that time was that she had gone back to my house and told my parents I had left her to walk home on her own. They took her home, but were angry with me when I came home; they told me I shouldn't leave a girl to walk home on her own. As far as I was concerned, she had decided to walk to the fair on her own, thinking that no-one would be meeting her there, and no-one would be walking her home afterwards - it was her choice to have to walk home alone. As a general rule, I would never have someone walk home alone, but back then I wouldn't stop what I was doing to walk someone home. At the time when she approached me at the fair, I didn't think about how she'd got there or how she was going to get home; all I thought about was how I wasn't going to spend time with her, because I had told her I wasn't seeing her that evening. It wasn't long after this that our relationship ended. I couldn't handle someone who always wanted to be around me. I wanted someone there when I wanted to spend time with them and have them leave me alone when I wanted to do my own thing. Writing this now I feel like I am portraying myself as arrogant and self-centred, but that definitely isn't how I would have seen or described myself. But it may have been how I came across at times.

One thing that used to confuse me when I was a teenager, and still does today, was my recognition (or lack of it) of people. I knew people in school, and yet if I saw them out of school - where I wasn't necessarily expecting to see them and out of school uniform - I wouldn't recognise them, even if they spoke to me. Yet, there are other times when I could recognise them without them saying a word. I seemed to do better recognising people when I could see them walking, than when I was face to face with them, interacting with them. There was a time I came home with my mum and brothers, and a friend of mine was waiting for me outside the house. It was during the summer holidays, so he wasn't in school uniform; he also hadn't shaved, and so had some stubble. I don't think until this point I had realised how often this friend needed to shave. As I got out of the car, he started speaking to me. I had no idea what he was saying, because I didn't think I knew him so I wasn't paying any attention. I smiled politely and walked straight past him. He continued to talk to me, and followed me down the drive towards the front door. I continued to pay no attention to him. Then, one of my brothers who had just got out of the car started talking to him and engaging him in conversation. I suddenly recognised him when I looked at the two of them talking. At this point, I engaged in conversation as if I had known who he was the whole time. I didn't want him to think I was weird in some way for not knowing my own friend, whom I saw every single day at school. I still get this as an adult where I don't recognise people I know very well.

At home, I had three younger brothers, but I didn't feel like I went out of my way to engage with any of them unless I was babysitting, where so the role I was playing was to 'look after' them like a babysitter would. In that situation, I did what was expected of me, but the focus for me was always on what I wanted to do. So when I was a teenager babysitting, the main thing I would do was to go swimming with my brothers - not because I thought they would enjoy swimming, but because that was what I wanted to do. Luckily, I think they did enjoy going swimming. This would be something we would do almost every day of the summer holidays. Mum would give me £5 to babysit my brothers for the day, and I would spend it on all four of us going to Arundel outdoor swimming pool, and getting some chips to share for lunch. If I had enough left over, I would buy myself *Nintendo Magazine* to read by the pool.

As a teenager, my bedroom often looked untidy. It was a mess in some ways, but well organised in other ways. I liked things to be tidy, but had a different view of 'tidiness' to my parents. I didn't particularly care if clothes were on the floor, but I liked things where I could find them and in my order. So books were stacked how I wanted them - everything had a place. I also felt my room, which wasn't actually that large, was too big for me. It didn't feel enclosed enough, so I had my bed with its side against a wall and the head of the bed under the window, then I put a chest of drawers at the end of the bed with things stacked up on the drawers, a wardrobe against the side of my bed with things stacked on top of it, too. I only left a small gap to squeeze through, and had a computer desk with a TV, video recorder and other things stacked on there, so that the space I had was now only the size of a single bed. I had black curtains to keep the light out. I liked being in the dark. I liked making dens that I could hide in, and would often crawl under my bed as it was even more comfortable than being on it - even with all my furniture blocking out the rest of the room.

## Conjuring up calm and wonder

Through my teens, I remained interested in nature - specifically being out in the woods, or by the sea. I was also very interested in sea creatures, especially sharks, whales and dolphins. I liked other sea creatures, but these were my main focus. As a teenager, I was becoming increasingly interested in swimming and being underwater - I liked being like creatures that lived underwater. I started to buy video documentaries on sharks, whales and dolphins. I tried to design a device that would read the brainwave activity of dolphins as they interacted with different images of items, and their behaviours. My thinking was that their brainwaves could be recorded when they approached symbols for food, etc., and then maybe scientists could begin to create a way of communicating with them. I thought, if brainwaves and behaviour were monitored enough, then perhaps scientists would be able to start linking brainwave patterns with specific behaviours they saw taking place at the same time - and perhaps with specific whistles they used. Then, maybe an underwater synthesiser could be used to communicate back. I didn't know whether this was possible, but it was an idea I had and submitted to BBC's *Tomorrow's World* programme.

I was also interested in the giant squid and the fact that it had never been seen alive. I couldn't understand how it could never have been seen alive, when sperm whales could find and eat them frequently enough. I had seen a documentary where a camera was harpooned into the back of a great white shark, and I couldn't see why scientists couldn't just harpoon some cameras designed to withstand deep water - perhaps with air tanks attached which would inflate pouches to raise them back to the surface after it detached from the whale's back, and red lights to light up the area in front of the whale. My view was that the whale would find the giant squid, and the cameras would film what happened. It may not have produced the best footage, but it would have at least produced footage of some live giant squid.

For a large part of my teenage years, I was part of dolphin watch. I used to go to the beach every day and sit in my grandparents' beach hut, looking out over the sea for signs of dolphins swimming in the channel. The idea was that any dolphins I saw, I would report where I saw them, at what time, and in what direction they were swimming. I used to sit on my own for hours with a telescope and binoculars, just watching the sea. One day, one of my brothers joined me. I don't think he was so interested in what we were doing, but this day we got lucky: I saw a fin. Unfortunately, it wasn't a dolphin's fin. I was able to tell that straightaway - it was a shark's fin. I shouted to my brother, "Come on, come on, quick, quick!" I grabbed the small dinghy we had and ran down towards the water. My brother ran after me, unsure as to what I had seen. He kept asking me "What is it? What is it?" I was too busy running to the sea to bother answering him though. We jumped into the dinghy and both started paddling out. I didn't want to take my eyes off the fin, in case I lost where it was. After we had paddled out a little way, my brother still wanted to know what we were doing. Perhaps he thought I had seen a dolphin... I told him, "There's a shark, I am just trying to get to it!" Next second, he jumped out of the dinghy and waded quickly back to shore, as if what we were doing was a bad idea. Annoyingly, by the time I got out into deeper water, the shark had lowered completely under the water and I couldn't work out where it had gone.

Almost every year during my teens, I went to the Brighton Sealife Centre and for one year, my grandparents got me a yearly membership which meant I visited very frequently. What was better still, I received a magazine and other bits from them. I had read books by people who dived with sea creatures for a living and started to think about whether it was possible to grow up and do that as a job. I wondered what you had to do to be a marine biologist. I thought it must be a great job, because you are underwater with the sea life where it is quiet and peaceful, with no other people around - at worst, maybe just one or two other people. But, even then, you wouldn't have to talk with them, and then you'd get to write and analyse what you had been learning. It sounded like a job I could do that didn't involve too much interaction with other people. It seemed ideal.

All adults I knew who worked seemed to do jobs that involved people; many jobs seemed to place lots of importance on being able to behave appropriately with people. When we had to do work experience in school, many of the teenagers got work experience in shops, banks or restaurants - and other places where I would have fallen to pieces if I'd had to do those jobs. I don't think I would have lasted a day at that point in my life. I decided I wanted to go scuba diving for my work experience. I had only recently heard about scuba diving as the term for what these underwater people were doing on the various documentaries. I thought, if I wanted to be a marine biologist, I would need to know how to dive. I didn't get to scuba dive during my work experience, but they did take me out on dives, and working for a small company, I usually only saw one or two people a day. My days consisted of cleaning scuba gear, making cups of tea, sorting paperwork and learning about the different equipment. I loved the smell of the equipment, and the watery smell of cleaning the equipment after a dive. It always smelt so fresh.

This was the ideal choice of work experience for me because it had minimal interaction with people, other than me approaching them to ask about different equipment and how it worked. They were happy not to approach me; they would set me a task, like spending the morning cleaning the diving gear, and I would then clean the diving gear without needing supervision. The tasks weren't complicated - they were often things deemed as boring. These are usually the things I like to do, because they allow me to be on my own and in my own thoughts.

The scuba diving company felt I did really well and appeared very keen and knowledgeable, so they offered a discount for me to train with them. Thus, I took my Padi Open Water Diver training. It was one of the best things

I have done. I took the course during late autumn and into early winter, so much of the diving was very cold. The first diving experience was in an indoor heated swimming pool. This was warm and comfortable, and allowed us students to get used to the diving equipment and to do all aspects of what we would have to do to pass the course. We had to dive in a freshwater lake. This was very cold, and I think it felt colder than it usually perhaps would have done, because we had to change into our scuba gear beside the lake and then walk in and swim out a little way to be in deeper water. When you drop backwards off a boat, all the water floods into the wetsuit at once, and your body warms the water now next to your skin. On the other hand, when you walk in from the shore, cold water slowly seeps in, filling the suit more and more with each step. It is always easier to dive straight into a swimming pool rather than climbing down the stairs into the pool, or lowering yourself into the water; much like it is easier to run and dive into the sea, rather than slowly walking in, then reaching that point where you go up on tiptoes and breathe in and tense your stomach muscles as a wave approaches.

Not only was diving in the lake very cold, but it was also very murky. The bottom of the lake had a thick layer of silt; as we lowered to the bottom, I could feel my legs reach the silt. It was a strange feeling. The silt felt incredibly soft, and my legs just continued to sink deeper and deeper. I remember wondering as I was lowering down whether it was possible to lower so far into the silt that I could get stuck and be unable get back out. It wasn't an anxiety wonder - just a curiosity wonder. The water was an opaque light greenish-brown colour. I noticed that light was passing through the water, and I could see bits floating, but visibility was probably no more than thirty centimetres.

In this lake, we had to run through each of the tests we were going to be doing out in the sea - for example, having our air turned off without notice, and then having to slowly rise to the surface whilst breathing out the whole time, at a speed no faster than the instructor's hand which was above our heads. We couldn't see the hand, though, as the instructor was behind us. I had no problem doing any of this. I found the whole experience of being underwater deeply relaxing and calming. I loved the quiet peacefulness of diving.

When it came to our main dive out to sea, it was a windy day in late October. We left the River Arun in a small Rigid Inflatable Boat (RIB) and travelled five miles out from the shore of Littlehampton, before coming to a halt. A line was thrown down, which we would follow and not let go of. We were told that there was a strong current out there; if we let go of the line even for a split second, we may have moved and been unable to find the line again. We could raise to the surface anywhere. There were three of us doing the diving course - two adults and myself. Both adults were sick before leaving the boat... and once they were in the water. The waves were large and rough; whenever the boat ended up between waves, you could no longer see the shore. I had no problem with this. One of the two adults really didn't want to dive now. They were scared of the water being too rough and of accidentally letting go of the line, but the instructor calmed them down and they went through with the dive.

The instructor warned us about basking sharks, telling us how they swim along with their mouths wide open. They wouldn't harm us on purpose, but if we happened to swim into one, we could easily swim into its open mouth before realising we had done so. You may wonder how you could be in the water with the world's second largest fish and not see it - well, when I dropped back off the boat into the water and started to lower under the water, I found out how that could be possible. Visibility wasn't great. I was only able to see my hand in front of my face if I actually placed it on my face mask. Even a centimetre from the mask, and I couldn't make it out. For me, this was great; it was like sensory deprivation. Above the water, it was windy, noisy. There was rain, and lots of movement on the boat - and even in the water, just bobbing up and down in the waves.

We had to go down ten metres. As I lowered, it got quieter and calmer. The first thing to go once I went completely underwater was all of the noise. All I could hear was the sound of my breathing and the bubbles rising from me. Then, a little further down, the waves changed - from something you could feel very clearly moving you each time, to just feeling a light pressure on one side of the body. Then there was a moment of no pressure - or perhaps it was a feeling of the pressure no longer increasing, and then a releasing of pressure, almost like a pressure now on the other side of my body. Then, at the bottom, even this seemed to stop. All I was aware of was peace, floating just above the bottom of the seafloor. It took what seemed like no time at all for my body to warm the cold water in my suit to body temperature, so I didn't feel hot or cold. Floating there, it felt like I had no sensory input other than the sound of my breathing.

It felt like I was relaxing under the water for ages before it was my turn to have my air turned off. I remember swimming to the surface with no air, just breathing out in one long continuous breath, rising no faster than the instructor's hand. I could notice the surface getting closer, and everything getting lighter. At that moment, I also noticed I was coming to the end of my breath. I only just made it to the surface at the speed I was breathing out, before I ran out of air. I was aware that if the surface was half a metre higher, I would have stopped breathing before breaking through. This made me feel that I would want to practice breathing out like this more often, to get used to breathing out over specific distances. The instructor was really impressed with me - he told me how well I did and how natural I seemed to find it all, and that I could easily become a diving instructor.

I had never actually thought of that as a job, until this moment. All of a sudden, I thought about the qualification I had just been through and thought about whether I would have been happy to do all of those things. There was only a small group of people taking the course, and most of it was underwater, so there wasn't lots of interaction with people. I thought maybe it was something I could do. The opportunity almost presented itself. Two of my relatives who lived in America were planning on sailing around the world and stopping off in the UK. They were visiting their grandparents over here in the UK when I spoke to them. Mum had told them about how I had just learnt to dive and the instructor felt I could go on to become a diving instructor. They said perhaps I would be interested in sailing around the world with them, teaching diving and taking people out on dives at different places where we'd stop off. Of course, I was very interested in this. I didn't think about money - like how much I would earn. I didn't care whether I was going to earn any money or not. My first thoughts were that there would be costs involved in me being on board - I would need food, etc. - so it made sense that I would do something that would earn enough money to cover the cost of me being on the boat. They were planning on sailing around the world a couple of years later, so I had time to get all of my diving qualifications before they arrived back in the UK to pick me up. Unfortunately, it never happened. A storm hit America where their boat was and damaged it beyond repair. I ended up leaving school and having to work - I never did have the opportunity to complete my diving qualifications.

Through the whole of my teens, I loved swimming. I went swimming as often as I could. I loved being in the water, the feeling of the surface of the water against my skin. I would rest my head in the water so that I could feel the surface tension against the side of my face - or I would have my hands slightly out of the water to feel the surface tension against my hands. I loved how my heart rate changed when I fully submerged myself. I used to dive down to the bottom of the swimming pool in Littlehampton and hold on to the bottom rail of the steps, sitting on the floor, and would just relax. It felt like I could stay underwater for ages without feeling like I was trying hard to hold my breath. I remember thinking I could breathe to some extent underwater to keep myself down longer. Whether this was just placebo, or something that actually worked, I don't know, but I would make all the motions as if I was breathing normally except for actually letting air in - I knew that breathing in water was definitely not something I wanted to do. I felt like this satisfied the breathing reflex to some extent, because I was 'breathing'. I also felt that this perhaps circulated and mixed the air more in my lungs, rather than maybe having all the carbon dioxide sinking down into the bottom of my lungs and the oxygen being up in my throat. I have continued to love swimming and being in water through to adulthood, and can lose track of time in water. I can get into a bath and think twenty minutes have passed, and get out to find that three or four hours have actually elapsed.

Even being in the swimming pool itself made me feel relaxed. As a child and teenager I usually got to go swimming when all other children were also around. In my later teens and adulthood, I was able to go at times when children and teens weren't around so much. But for most of the time, changing rooms were horrible places; they were noisy and crowded, and the only way to feel slightly free from all the chaos was to get one of the cubicles, but these weren't always free. Besides, if you were going into the pool, rather than coming out and changing before going home, the time it would take to get a free cubicle, change, then find a locker meant enduring more of the chaos than just finding a locker, zoning out and focusing on changing as quickly as possible - having arrived at the swimming centre with swimming trunks already on under my clothes.

Once out of the changing room you would enter the hectic, loud, chaotic swimming pool area where every sound echoes. There is something comforting I find in echoes, but when the pool area is too busy, the comforting effects of the echo just aren't enough. The strange thing was, being in this amount of chaos and unpleasantness actually made the feeling of entering the water - putting my ears under the water and closing my eyes - for the first time even more pleasant, as if somehow the relief or escape from the sights and sounds brought more calm than if I'd walked into a quiet changing room and then into a quiet pool.

This is a bit like what I would do with hypnosis for people who struggle to relax. I may suggest they take a moment to tense a body part up, as I'd count to three, and then let it relax. Then, I would count really slowly and they'd hold the tension, wishing they could just stop and relax; when I'd eventually get to three, and they could finally release the tension, they'd relax much deeper than if I were to say "focus on this body part and just let it gently relax".

I have always liked solving problems and designing things. I'm not so good at making things - I seem to do alright at construction, but I have never been confident at using tools. If I do try something new, like using a tool, or trying to make something, I like to do it on my own privately - I don't like to be seen doing it until I know I can do it well. I don't have to excel at something to be comfortable doing it in public, but I have to be proficient enough that I think I am doing at least an average job. As a teenager, a friend and I used to design tree camps and death slides. I also used to make secret camps in the sand dunes at the beach. I never thought about these things as being co-operative or working as a team. We would work alongside each other - we would have our tasks and would get on with what we had to do. I never saw it as playing. I didn't know how play would come into making tree camps or death slides. The idea of building a tree camp was that it gave us somewhere to go to hang out, and the death slide was a quick way to the bottom. I used to like sitting alone in the tree camp. In the winter, it was warmer in the tree camp than just sitting in a tree. It was relaxing to sit in the warmth of the camp, just listening to birds singing, and the sound of leaves rustling in the trees, and creaking branches as they swayed in the breeze. And when it rained, you could listen to the rain as it hit the roof of the tree camp and the Perspex windows.

Unlike many people I have known over the years, I loved magic. I was fascinated by magic. I knew it was fake - I mean, I knew a card didn't vanish, and that it was somehow palmed or moved elsewhere. But this was what impressed me. I wanted to know how the trick was done - even a simple answer would be interesting, because the magician had to do that simple answer under people's noses. My question was always: what did they do to make sure the trick wasn't seen?

I attended a school reunion in 2014, and the first thing the first person I saw at the reunion said was: "What I remember about you was you were always into weird things - you always carried a magic book on you and wanted to talk about magic, and you still seem to be into all the same stuff now." This is true, I love magic as an adult as much as I ever have. When I was a teenager, I used to try to learn different magic tricks from different magic sets and books on magic. I used to try to design my own tricks. What I struggled with was how to create an atmosphere for the illusion. I could read the steps of how to do a trick in a book; I could then practice those exact steps in front of a mirror and master them. I used to find dexterous processes difficult to master, but with practice I could do most things. But I had no 'showmanship'. I would say what a book told me to say and, like a robot, I would do what I had to do. But when I came to perform tricks in front of family members, they wouldn't be fooled. I couldn't misdirect them - I struggled with timing misdirection. Magic is like music, you see - it is all about the beats and the spaces between the beats. It is about tension and relaxation. Magic was the ideal interest for someone who loved designing things, and problem-solving, but my view is that you also need to understand social communication. That doesn't mean you need to be good in social communication situations, but you need to understand how to direct attention - you need to value the importance of directing attention and the timing of it. To do this, you need to be able to engage an audience. I wasn't good at engaging an audience, because engagement is a two-way communication process. I was often talking at an audience, not engaging with it.

You can notice this in lessons or lectures you have attended. There are some lecturers who are great at engaging the audience: they may be just talking to the audience and not having a two-way dialogue, but they talk to the audience in such a way that you feel involved in their lecture. Other lecturers may convey the same information, but you find their lectures flat and perhaps difficult to sit through because you feel talked at for the duration of the lecture, rather than engaged with. Despite trying, I have never mastered showmanship. I can learn the behaviours, but I am going through an intentional mental pattern, so if I need everyone to be looking in one place when I palm a card elsewhere, then I need to know exactly what I am supposed to say or do at that moment, as part of the time sequence for that stage in the trick.

I have continued to be fascinated with magic. I read about magic and watch magic shows, but I don't often try to learn magic tricks anymore. Other than wanting to show my 'magic uncle' what I had learnt, and putting on magic shows for him, I have never wanted to be a performer. I liked doing tricks I had learnt in front of people - not to 'perform', as such, but to say "look what I have just learnt, isn't it interesting".

Many of my relatives are very musical, so I have always been interested in the idea of playing musical instruments, but I seem to find it difficult to learn dexterous actions, and to link what goes on intellectually with physical actions. I have always felt what is needed is to get 'myself' out of the way and just let 'it' happen. Oddly, the things I like most in music are the spaces between notes. When listening to instruments like cellos or violins and other 'sliding' instruments, there is a moment when the movement stops, before it slides back the other way. This is the moment I like. I tried to learn many different musical instruments as a teenager. I had guitar lessons and trombone lessons; I used to regularly try to play piano, but I was never able to grasp the instruments. Music teachers said in my school reports that I seemed natural with music, but I never felt natural. Now I am older, I think it was partly in how I was trying to learn and how I was taught. I was always taught having to read sheet music and play what I was reading. Although I can understand sheet music slowly - and if I have been trying to play a piece of music for a

122

while I can understand it faster - I have never been able to read the music at speed like I can read a book, and I can never link written marks with specific actions that will make certain sounds.

The songs I can play on a piano (not very well, but I have remembered them with minimal instruction and can still play them when I decide to, over thirty years later) were taught by someone showing me how to play the tune, and then me copying their actions so that I am learning exactly what I need to do. There were no extra steps, like having to read the music, process this, and then play the music. I think this is how I learn best. Not just with music - but with most physical activities. When I learn, I try to imagine myself being the other person and try to mimic them so that I am doing exactly the same as them. I usually have to do this slowly at first, but as I get used to it, I can improve. This is one of the difficulties with schools; frequently, they teach the whole class in the same way, and although nowadays there is more focus on multi-sensory learning and ensuring everyone is able to learn through their preferred modality, I think this is often too simplistic. People may learn best visually, but that doesn't necessarily mean 'reading' or seeing images - it could be watching demonstrations and being free to walk around to get the best angle, and to then copy the teacher.

The one instrument which I seemed to naturally 'get' was one which I have only played once, but in that one instance, the music teacher asked if I had had lessons: a drum kit. We only had a chance to play drums once in school in a music lesson, and I definitely didn't have permission to play drums out of school. I remember hitting each drum once to see what each sounded like;

then, I just hit the drums to make rhythms. I have never played drums since that one time over 25 years ago, but I can possibly understand why I may have got on better playing the drums than other instruments - because I like rhythms and patterns, and don't like mismatches in rhythms or patterns. I also tap a lot, and as a teenager I used to tap far more often. I copy rhythms or patterns I hear, like bird sounds, the ways people put cutlery on a table, or the pattern of car doors being shut when people exit their car, and patterns in certain phrases that people say.

There are some things I learn best from copying; other things, meanwhile, I can learn well from reading. I personally rarely learn from enforced discussions, yet many courses will say student discussions and debates are important to learning. As a teenager, and still as an adult, I was happier to watch how someone does something, copy them, and be able to ask that expert questions if there was something I didn't understand, or if there was more I felt I needed to know. For more academic subjects, meanwhile, I would learn best from reading, and then talking about what I had learnt with others - or more specifically, *at* others. I like others asking me questions, but it has to be all about stimulating my thinking further. I struggle with enforced discussions like "how does this ... relate to you?", "discuss what you think the implications are to the field of ...", "discuss how you feel about...", or "discuss your understanding of...".

Any of these rigid discussion topics would have me closing down straight away. I would be unable to link these questions with what I was learning. Someone starting a very general discussion with me, however, asking me perhaps what have I been learning about a subject, is likely to be able to lead me to answer some of these questions by starting general and gradually becoming more specific. This normally comes from a one-to-one talk with someone, not a group discussion. I would have nothing to prove to anyone about what I know or don't know, so in discussion groups I was unlikely to contribute anything. I would be listening and picking up on anything that interested me as additional knowledge, but I would never feel any compulsion to contribute. I didn't care if I disagreed with what people were saying - I didn't feel a need to express that, as it was of no interest to me what others believed. I was always more of an observer than a participant.

The event that transformed my life happened in 1993. The ITV television channel aired a programme called *The Hypnotic World of Paul McKenna*. The show was essentially a televised version of stage hypnosis. I had never seen hypnosis before and, watching the show, I didn't really understand what it was. Paul would say that he couldn't show the actual hypnotic induction on TV, but all these people on stage were hypnotised. It appeared that all the people on the show did exactly as he asked them to do. When people did some of the things they were asked to do - like being asked to become astronauts - they seemed to take on what they were asked to do as if it was real to them. I remember wondering whether this hypnosis thing would be able to make people learn different skills, by becoming people with those skills... I didn't know how it worked, I had never seen hypnosis before, and had still never seen how to hypnotise someone.

Another aspect that interested me was that these people seemed to do whatever Paul asked them to do. It looked like he somehow had control over them. To me, as a teenager, I started thinking that this was something I needed to learn. I wanted to know how to hypnotise teachers and other children in school, to get them to do what I wanted them to do. I thought about what it must be like to walk into a classroom and hypnotise everyone in the room, so that they were all quiet and so that the teacher would teach what I wanted to know about - without having to move on with what they were supposed to be teaching, and without other children in the class interrupting or being annoying while I was trying to learn what I wanted to learn.

I thought hypnosis might be the ultimate way of controlling the world around me so that people left me alone when I wanted to be left alone, and so that I didn't have to do things I didn't want to do. If a teacher asked me to do something I didn't want to do, say, I would be able to hypnotise them and tell them they wouldn't make me do that. At this point, I had only watched the stage hypnosis TV shows; I hadn't learnt anything about hypnosis. My views of what it was and the power of hypnosis were entirely based on my judgements and interpretations of Paul McKenna clicking his fingers, saying 'sleep', then telling people what to do and when to do it. I don't remember ever thinking it was fake, whereas growing up, I have met many people who say to me they think hypnosis is all fake, and people on these hypnosis stage shows must all be stooges. That thought never crossed my mind, but I did have a very naive and incorrect view of what hypnosis was, because I was basing my initial views on what I had watched on TV.

Obviously, and tantalisingly, it didn't reveal how to do the hypnosis - it only showed the results of people being hypnotised. I remember thinking about the *Star Wars* films and the Jedi using The Force and wondering whether it was done like that. I really wanted to know how it was done.

I set out to see if there were any books I could read on hypnosis to learn how to do it. I couldn't find anything in the local library, and it seemed difficult to find any hypnosis books in bookshops. A part of this lack of success finding books that would give me answers was frustrating, but at the same time this made me more curious. I wondered why there were no books on hypnosis... Was it some big secret thing, so powerful that they didn't want people to know how to do it? They wouldn't show or talk about how to do it on the TV programme - so maybe it was something that only the privileged few could learn. The harder I found it to find any information about how to do hypnosis, the more curious I became about the subject.

Eventually, after searching for a while in different bookshops, I found a self-hypnosis book and tape set. This set had a book explaining what hypnosis was and gave different inductions to use for hypnosis, and wording for suggestions to overcome different problems. Then, the cassette tape had two relaxation self-hypnosis sessions on it. The book was very simplistic in its explanations of what hypnosis was, and my first thoughts were that there was something special about the words in the book - I felt that to hypnotise someone, I would have to read the words exactly as they were written. It said to read the words in a monotonous voice, which for me wasn't a problem - that was how I spoke already. But it wasn't how I saw Paul McKenna speak on his show.

This was in the days long before YouTube. There were only four TV channels, and there was only this one hypnosis programme for me to go by - and my one cassette tape. The hypnosis on the cassette tape was monotonous and very direct in the language it used: it said things like "you will now…", "you are now…", and told me what I was now experiencing, which wasn't necessarily what I was experiencing. I didn't find the hypnosis on the cassette tapes very effective. My view was that they seemed to get it wrong. If someone was telling me what I was feeling, and I wasn't feeling what they said I was feeling, then they were incorrect. If they were incorrect about this, then did hypnosis really work? If hypnosis was as powerful as I was imagining it being from what I had seen on TV, then if a hypnotist said, "You are now deeply relaxed and you can see a beautiful garden", this is what I expected my experience to be. I expected to be deeply relaxed looking out over a beautiful garden, not feeling 'a bit relaxed' and seeing darkness.

At this point in time, this was the only book I had found on hypnosis, and I was disappointed with most of what I read. It didn't match at all with the hypnosis I had seen on TV. It didn't explain about what I could see being done. There was nothing in the book about influencing others - about being able to say to someone "when I say your name you are going to suddenly find yourself stuck in your chair, unable to move". The one thing that was in the book which I almost completely overlooked was the suggestions to give people to overcome problems. I had never thought about people having problems, like anxiety or low self-esteem; I just thought people were people, and the anxiety I felt in specific situations was just normal for me - not something that anyone could change. The assumption made in this book, however was that you could change parts of who you are. At this point, I had never heard about counselling, or psychotherapy, and this book was the first time I had heard of a subject called psychology - but I still thought that there was very specific wording you needed to use to do different things in hypnosis. I didn't know where or how the author of this book had learnt hypnosis, but I assumed there must be somewhere you could learn it. I was sure it wasn't a school subject, because I had never heard it mentioned in school or in lessons, and I thought the hypnosis scripts in the book were worded with the exact words needed to achieve what the script was about. I thought about hypnosis in the same way I thought about magic spells.

Through my teens, and into my early twenties, I had been interested in the occult, ghosts, and many other paranormal subjects (and I still enjoy these subjects now, but my views and thinking have evolved and developed over the years). To me, reading a self-hypnosis book that had hypnosis scripts reminded me of books of magic spells and rituals. With these spells and rituals, I believed the wording and processes were the exact steps you had to take - like having to put a machine together correctly for it to work. To me, it was not something you could change and adapt - in the same way you couldn't put a machine together 'any old way' and expect it to work. I couldn't relate to any of the problems mentioned in the self-hypnosis book, so I found them of no use or interest to me at that time. I did, however, try out some of the hypnotic inductions on my brothers and on my mum. I had no way of knowing if they had worked. I assumed I had done hypnosis correctly, because I had read exactly what was written down, exactly as it said to read it - but I didn't have them acting like frogs, or pretending to be astronauts.

It was another hypnosis program of Paul McKenna's - a documentary called *Paul McKenna's Secrets of Hypnosis* - that suddenly opened my eyes to hypnosis and to understanding hypnosis in a more realistic way. The documentary started with Paul talking about his stage show, and talking about what was coming up on the show, including someone being cured of a fear of flying standing on the open back of a flying aeroplane, speed reading, overcoming pain, and much more. Paul explained a bit about what hypnosis was and how it worked, in such a way that made me realise it wasn't necessarily all about the exact words. He explained that he couldn't reveal how someone was being hypnotised on TV, but he could reveal some of what the hypnotist looks for when they are hypnotising someone.

Paul then went on to explain various signs that the person is changing state and entering a hypnotic trance. The camera panned in close on the person being hypnotised, and showed various signs like eye movement under the eye lids, reddening of the face, muscles relaxing, breathing slowing down and becoming deeper. These may sound like small points, but being told that the hypnotist is watching for certain signs meant to me that it wasn't so much that there were specific scripts or words to use to do hypnosis, but that the words used needed to be able to somehow achieve the changes sought. Paul explained that, when people get absorbed in something - "like watching this programme" - they shut out everything else. They forget about the wallpaper, they forget about the TV stand, and pictures on the walls, and all furniture. The only thing they are aware of is the TV programme, and if that TV programme is engaging enough, you suspend belief as you also get drawn into the reality created by the programme. So, if something scary happens on the programme, you can jump and be scared, even though what you are experiencing isn't real. Paul described how this was just like doing hypnosis and being hypnotised.

To me, what Paul had done was reveal how hypnotic inductions were supposed to work. It wasn't about the words specifically; it was about creating this state in people. I still didn't really have the skills or confidence to do this, but I now knew and understood what I needed to learn. I also realised that it was largely about observing people closely. I had never noticed people's breathing before, or changes to facial colour, unless they went very red from embarrassment or from doing something energetic. I realised that I was going to have to learn a lot more about people, behaviour and body language, and was going to have to watch people with intent to see what I could learn about them.

On the documentary, they had someone talking about cults, techniques used by cults, and how these techniques are essentially hypnosis. They had someone demonstrate using eye contact and gestures to convey an assertive message, and demonstrated language politicians use to manipulate and influence people. I had watched many documentaries - I loved watching documentaries - but I hadn't watched anything that had an impact on me anywhere near as much as this one did. Paul managed to keep his hand in ice cold water without feeling any pain while thinking about a memory; someone had managed to get rid of a skin condition through a number of hypnosis sessions; different people were cured of phobias rapidly with hypnosis; children had their immune systems boosted using imagination... All of this made me start to wonder what the human mind was capable of. I started to wonder whether I could use hypnosis on myself to do different things.

Firstly, I hypnotised one of my brothers to be better at playing pool. I found a snooker improvement script and just swapped the word snooker for pool and made a few other small changes to suit my brother - and it worked. He improved his pool playing. Then, I hypnotised one of my brothers to stop wetting the bed, and that worked as well. I didn't use a script from a book for that, but I took a script from a second self-hypnosis book I had bought. I'd read through the inductions, picking one I thought my brother would like, then read through the scripts for treating different problems and found bits from the different scripts that I thought could be relevant. To those, I added a few ideas of my own, and read that script to him. These early successes gave me the confidence to start writing scripts for myself.

As I learnt more about hypnosis, I began to also learn more about rapport. I had never heard about rapport before, but it was mentioned a lot in hypnosis books. Prolonged eye contact, like a 'hypnotic gaze', was mentioned. This initially confused me. I had assumed that people spent all their time when talking with each other staring at each other. "Look at me when I'm talking to you" is a common phrase to hear. Suddenly, I was reading of hypnotists saying "look into my eyes".

Why would they need to tell people to look into their eyes, if they were already looking into their eyes? The implication was that people aren't actually always looking into each other's eyes. I decided to watch people, and what I noticed was that there was a pattern to eye contact - it wasn't all or nothing. People don't stare at each other like I assumed they must do; rather, they make eye contact for about five seconds, then they look away for a few seconds, then back again for about five seconds. When someone is trying to state something that is important to them, they hold eye contact for longer. When someone likes another person, they make eye contact with that person for longer during conversations - but they often seem to make less eye contact when they like someone and that person is looking back at them. People seemed to look away when they were thinking about things, before responding to what was said, and they start looking away just before the other person has finished talking.

All of this intrigued me. There were patterns to eye contact that perhaps I could learn. It made sense that a hypnotist would want to make prolonged eye contact, because prolonged eye contact got attention and was hard to ignore. But the meaning of the eye contact seemed to depend on the situation. As a teenager, I didn't have the skills for mentally keeping track of this level of detail, especially not during conversations, so I stuck to what seemed to be about right, which was to make eye contact with people (well, nearly make eye contact - I actually found it more comfortable to look through people, which is still what I usually do) for about five seconds. I would count these in my head, and then break eye contact for about five seconds, and just follow this pattern.

I also started to notice how people had personal space. I disliked people standing too close to me. I would go inside myself when people stood close to me, but I didn't really get the difference between someone standing close to me because they wanted to be affectionate, someone standing close to me because we had to line up and stand close, and someone standing close to me because they were wanting to intimidate me and perhaps hit me. This meant that, externally, I was generally unresponsive. I would go inside my mind regardless of the person's reason for standing where they did. I never wanted to stand close to people, but I would want to touch soft materials. I would reach for people's clothes, or touch people's coats, if they were soft, as I walked past their chair perhaps - and I wouldn't think about the consequences of this. Understanding people had personal space meant I began to see patterns when watching others, and I could learn from these.

It is surprising that you don't see what you don't know to look for, and then when you do see it you wonder how you never managed to spot it before. Since being an adult, and starting to read books on the subject, I have found myself disagreeing with much of what I see written about body language - but reading into it was definitely a good place to start. There was information about different facial expressions - about how there is a difference between a 'genuine' smile and a 'fake' smile (it comes down to the muscles around the eyes that create crow's feet when you smile). So I started practicing smiling involving these muscles in front of a mirror, because I wanted to be able to smile convincingly, especially when I hadn't 'got' a joke or when I wasn't really interested in something someone was saying but I knew I should politely listen along. I learnt about different hand gestures and how they could mark things out or reveal more information, and about how they could be calming or aggressive, inviting or dismissive.

All of this came from my interest in hypnosis, and as I continued to learn about hypnosis, I was finding that hypnosis is actually just about having advanced rapport-building skills - interesting for someone who needed to develop their most definitely not advanced rapport-building skills. My mum had sent off for a free hypnosis introductory tape from a company offering training to become a hypnotherapist. Mum was also becoming interested in this idea of being a hypnotherapist, so we had both listened to and read the materials sent through. I had also bought two Paul McKenna books, one teaching what hypnosis was and how to do hypnosis, and - unlike other hypnosis books I had read - Paul's book spoke highly of Dr Milton Erickson, and also spoke about neuro-linguistic programming (NLP). Other hypnosis books seemed to gloss over Dr Erickson's contribution to hypnosis, dismissing it as not really being about hypnosis. Prior to *The Hypnotic World of Paul McKenna*, all books described a totally different type of hypnosis. They described an approach to hypnosis I would now know is called authoritarian or classical hypnosis, whereas Paul's book spoke of modern hypnosis, and described modern hypnosis as being Dr Milton Erickson's approach (known as Ericksonian hypnosis) and NLP. This book described hypnotic communication as being an input from what the hypnotist observed about the client or subject, about their behaviour, what they said and how they said it; this input would lead to the hypnotist giving some output in the form of words and behaviours, which would become the input for the subject. Then, their response to what the hypnotist said and did would become the output that the hypnotist would pick up on as the new input, and this would cycle around. So it was a fluid process, not about hypnosis scripts, but about learning to pay attention to others and to communicate with others in a meaningful way.

What I was reading about Dr Milton Erickson was about how he used observations as a fundamental part of his hypnosis and therapy. He believed that most of our communication was unconscious, so by closely watching non-verbal behaviour whilst listening to someone talking, you could get this extra information about what they were truly thinking and feeling. This non-verbal behaviour is usually the honest part of the person, so when someone says yes with a smile on their face, but they shake their head, the shaking head - being done unconsciously - is most likely to be the honest answer to the question, not the smile and the word 'yes'.

I always say hypnosis is the thing that helped me learn to communicate. As a teenager, I still said and did things wrong, and would take things too literally. But I now had a path. I believe many children with Asperger's are no different to me, in that they are intelligent and able to learn, but they just don't know what they need to be learning or where or how to find it out. I don't think parents of those children know where their children can go to learn the skills they need. I have said to many people with Asperger's that hypnosis helped me with it, and some people I know have tried hypnotherapy for themselves, and felt that it never helped them. Then, I have often explained that it wasn't using hypnosis in itself (although as an adult, I have used hypnosis to help in some areas), but it was *learning about hypnosis* that has helped. To become good at hypnosis, you have to learn to observe people - to be able to copy people's behaviours, to be able to use your behaviour to influence the behaviours of others. You have to learn to excel at communication skills, and to recognise patterns of behaviour and what different behaviour might mean, and then how to test your theories.

Whilst in school I never became able to manipulate teachers and other students into doing much of what I wanted, but I did realise that behaviours, like how I had been influencing other children since primary school - for example, by suggesting ideas and then waiting for the idea to come from someone seemingly more influential - was actually doing hypnosis. I started to get on a little better in school, because I could make 'normal'-looking eye contact which helped me to fit in more. I still didn't care about most of what others said - it didn't interest me at all - and I still struggled to recall what people had spoken to me about unless it was something I was interested in. But in the moment, I could now fake looking interested.

Hypnosis gave me skills I could use as well. When I used to play manhunt at night, I would use synaesthesia so that I could see sounds. This helped me to know where other children were, because whenever they moved I would see a flash of light coming from their location. I enjoyed the TV series *Quantum Leap* during my teens, and identified with Dr Sam Beckett as a role model due to his leaping through time from one life to the next and fixing people's problems, all the while remaining anonymous. I liked the idea of helping people but not taking credit for it - not being in the limelight. In one episode of *Quantum Leap*, Sam is playing pool and he has a hologram projected onto the pool table consisting of a dot on the white ball showing where he needs to hit the ball with the cue; there is also a dot on the object ball he needs to hit with the cue ball, and a line showing the path the object ball will take. I used to do this, but imaginarily, to help me with my pool playing. I also managed to convince my teachers for physical education to allow me to play pool in all of my PE lessons. We had been asked what sport we wanted to do for our PE lessons, and the idea was that the sport we chose, we would have to do each lesson.

Discovering hypnosis was definitely the defining moment of my teens for me. That was the thing that gave me the skills I needed to handle life. It took many years to get things right, but because I became obsessed with hypnosis straightaway, and wanted to know how to do it, I developed enough basic skills to successfully navigate through my last couple of years of secondary school and into young adulthood.

I have never been good at learning something and retaining it unless I saw a reason or had an interest in it. My view would be that all children should be taught hypnosis from a young age, especially children with Asperger's, because what is needed is to study how to communicate with people, how to 'read' the feedback you get, and what to say or do based on that feedback. It doesn't mean everything always works, or that it is always easy - but it can give you a good starting place. Even in my autism spectrum disorder assessment, the psychologist said I had 'impeccable non-verbal communication, but there were no facial expressions'; even now, as an adult I have to work at it. It can take years of practice and learning. I can do larger movements, but the more subtle the behaviour is that I am supposed to be doing, the harder it is to pull off.

All the while, I am essentially faking it and trying to do the response or behaviour that is correct for the situation by first working out what is correct for the situation - what combination of behaviours, how many different behaviours, gestures and body postures, small facial movements, appropriate eye movements, and so on... You see, this may be almost impossible to pull off during conversations, unless you are controlling the conversation, like in therapy sessions.

Dan Jones

# CHAPTER FIVE

## *Adulthood*

I left school at sixteen and got a job working at a holiday camp in Bognor Regis. What I really wanted to do at that age was find a way to do something where I was continually learning. I had written in my Record of Achievement that I wanted to become a marine biologist. I never felt like I had any difficulty with learning knowledge I was taught at school in most lessons, but I wasn't very good at getting coursework done unless it was about a subject that interested me. I would think to myself that I'd learnt the information in lessons, so why would I now want to waste my time doing coursework to let others know what I knew? I only put effort into the coursework when I was genuinely interested in the coursework I was doing - usually where the coursework itself was going to be a learning process for me around a subject I wanted to know more about.

I also wasn't very good at exams. Knowledge doesn't flow out of me very well when I am looking at questions on a page. Multiple choice questions often weren't worded the same way that I would word the answers, so I would struggle to understand which answer was correct. If someone asked me the question and engaged me in conversation, I would tell them the answer in my words, and they could question me further about my answer - this way, they would find that I know what I am talking about. I am also left-handed and have very untidy handwriting, as mentioned in a previous chapter. I have always been told my handwriting looks like a spider has crawled across my work, so in exams I would try to write neatly; of course, though, this would mean I'd take far longer to actually get anything written. As a result of not being good at exams or coursework, I didn't get very good GCSE grades. I was also told by my parents that you were supposed to get a job at sixteen, so after trying to find a job for a while, I finally ended up at Butlin's.

I can remember my first day. I got dressed up smart, with a shirt and tie. I had to go to a dimly-lit lecture theatre-type room. I walked into the room and saw all of these adults - who were also starting on the same day - sat in the chairs; none of them had dressed smart, none of them looked like they had made any effort to impress our new employer. We were spoken to about working at Butlin's and then told which departments we would be working in.

When applying for the job, you just applied to be a 'team member', and when you arrived, they placed you where they felt you would be best suited. I had done a paper round when I was in school, and I had done work experience for a scuba diving company, but I didn't really know what I would be good at, or what doing different jobs would be like. I knew I was scared of having to talk to people - I didn't feel I had the skills to do that. I had always thought I wouldn't be able to serve people in shops or restaurants. But I needed a job, so I was aware that I had to try to do whatever I was told I was doing. I was assigned to work in catering.

The first job I had in catering was clearing tables. I liked doing this job, because I had to clear the table; place the rubbish in the bin on a trolley; place the cutlery into a cutlery holder; plates, bowls and saucers on the trolley's shelves; and cups in trays on the top of the trolley. Once the table was cleared, I would then clean it and push the chairs in. I loved that I could spend hours each day in my own world in my mind, carrying out this same pattern. It was satisfying to clear all the tables in a section and look back and see everything neat and orderly.

Something that surprised me was how staff behaved. I thought that adults' work was serious. Yet staff would laugh and joke with each other. Most of the staff were serious in front of customers, and not all staff worked equally as hard, but staff seemed to want to interact with each other. I had imagined that you went to work, you focused on the job you had to do for the duration of your shift, then you went home. I didn't think that people interacted with their colleagues during their shift.

I got quite quick and efficient at clearing tables and stacking the trolley as full as possible. To me, it was almost like playing a game of Tetris. There were some issues though, which were gradually picked up. Being out on the venue floor meant that when things were quieter, other members of staff would want to have fun and joke around - and I wouldn't know what I was supposed to do or how I was supposed to behave. I tried to fake it and appear like I knew what I was doing, but inside, I was wishing that there was a way to escape. Many of my colleagues were kind, caring and supportive; people who always went out of their way to make me feel supported and included, whereas I was probably the serious one, and the main person I got on with was an elderly lady who worked on the trolleys, and had done so for many years. She didn't mess around, and was quiet and laid back, definitely someone I was more comfortable around.

I also found myself whistling and tapping while I was in my own little world doing my job, and I wouldn't notice customers wanting my attention. To be fair, even if I did notice them, I didn't want to talk to them, I wanted to avoid them. Sometimes I was asked to work on the tills if it was busy or if there weren't enough staff. At this point in my experience, this was the worst possible role for me. I wasn't very good at being given money and working out how much change I was supposed to give back, and even when I was using a till that let me enter what money I had been given so that I knew what change I needed to issue, I was still nervous about it. I was nervous about whether I was adding up the correct change from the till into my hand to give to the customer, and I would have to do all this under the pressure of having a queue of people all waiting to be served, and all obviously wanting me to be quick.

I have always had a problem with being able to remember the correct names for things. I frequently say words that come to my mind, and I know what I mean by that word, but I don't have the real word available to me to say or think of instead - even if I see the real word, it can take a moment for me to realise that is the real word. I am aware this can be frustrating for people who tell me that they don't understand what I am saying - I then say the same thing again but with more emphasis, hoping somehow that the other person would become a mind reader and work it out.

So I may see an egg on a plate and think 'flibble', and no matter how hard I try to think of the real word, it doesn't come to me. When using a till system which may have 100 different buttons labelled with things like 'egg', 'bacon', 'chips', 'orange squash', each button is still perhaps only about a centimetre square, though, so finding the word 'egg' when I can't even think of the word I am supposed to be looking at - and being under pressure to find it fast, because there is a queue of people staring at me waiting - gets really stressful. Although I have a lot of gadgets, I also have a fear of using things I'm not yet used to using, and even sometimes when I am used to using them, if they aren't mine, I worry about using them. So, when using a till, I worried that somehow I was going to press a wrong combination of buttons, or do something that would break the till, and then there was having to actually deal with the customers.

When working with customers there seems to be this odd perception that customers are always right, which is obviously wrong to me. I would put so much mental effort into serving a customer and making sure they had the correct change - checking and double-checking before I finally handed over the change - that if a customer said that I had given them the wrong change (that they had given me a £20 note, not a £10 note, and so I owed them an additional £10), then I would expect the till to be cashed up. If the till was £10 up, then they were correct and could have the £10; if the till was correct, then they were wrong and couldn't have £10. This would mean stopping the whole queue for many minutes, which obviously wasn't something managers wanted. There was added motivation to expect this - if the till was out at the end of the day the staff member using that till had to make up the difference from their wages, so making the till £10 down could result in the loss of over half a day's pay.

Eventually, I got my dream job at Butlin's. I was moved from working on the floor to the pot wash. The pot wash consisted of a large conveyor belt dishwashing machine with a counter at one end, onto which the trolleys were unloaded, and shelves and trolleys for cutlery, crockery, cups, saucers and tea and coffee pots at the other end. The pot wash was separate from the kitchen - it was a room all on its own - and generally, this pot wash was only for cleaning items from the restaurant floor, not pots and pans from the kitchen. People rarely came into the pot wash unless they were wheeling in a trolley. Even then, they would quickly unload it, pick up replacement trays for their trolley, before heading back out of the pot wash to continue clearing tables. There were two doors through which the trolleys went through: one that opened inwards so that they could push the trolleys into the pot wash; and one which opened outwards, for them to push the trolleys out through. There was also a door at the side which led out to the restaurant serving area - this was where I would carry out clean crockery, tea and coffee pots for the staff to serve onto. I would take clean cutlery, cups and saucers out the front doors from the pot wash; the trolleys used to refill these for customers to pick up after they had been served.

The pot wash was often hot and noisy, but I didn't mind. It felt so calm and peaceful once I turned the machine off between using it. I used to love these quiet times. I couldn't really hear what was going on out in the restaurant area or in the customer seating area, so when the machine was off, I was in a room all alone in silence. When the machine was running it was noisy, but it was a constant rhythmic noise. I would load and unload the machine in patterns. When loading the machine, my goal was to try to pack everything onto the machine as neatly and as tightly together as possible. I didn't want things overlapping, or being packed incorrectly, but I wanted to make it so that I was using the machine as efficiently as possible. This meant that I had to learn how the different items could fit together, and how I wanted the trolleys unloaded so that I didn't have to walk around the counter and get different bits from different areas - I wanted all plates together, all cups together, etc. As I got better at loading it, I increased the speed of the machine until I had reached full speed.

The challenge then was mastering the unloading. The conveyor belt would stop once items reached the other end of the machine, so my aim was to load the machine until either everything was on it, or until it reached the other end, whichever came first. Then, I would go to the unloading end, leave an item in place where it stopped the machine going, and would then clear away all the other items I could reach, before removing the item I had left stopping the conveyor belt; as all the remaining items came towards me, I would try to pack them away where they were supposed to go fast enough to prevent the conveyor belt coming to a halt. If there were two of us working in the pot wash, one of us would try to load the machine as quickly as possible, and one would be unloading quickly, so that the conveyor belt never stopped.

To unload the machine efficiently, I had to lay out where everything needed to go around me so that I could move as little as possible and put everything where it was supposed to go. It would slow me down if I had to step over to put things away, or had to walk around the machine. This was also why everything had to be loaded into the machine in a specific way, so that all dinner plates would come through at the same time, all cups would come through at the same time, etc. That way I could stand in one location, doing all of one type of thing - unloading all cups to one side of the machine, for example - and then move to the other side of the machine when the plates were coming through to unload them all to the other side of the machine. For me, working in the pot wash was the best actual job I have ever done. I was in a small room on my own, and I was doing something repetitive that would allow me to be in my own world in my mind. I liked devising ways to be more efficient, and I didn't have to worry about interacting with other people, especially customers.

The problems came when Butlin's would have busy periods and events that required staff to do roles they didn't normally do - or when changes would happen and I would have to do a different role. This used to terrify me. I would be asked to do things like being a waiter in the restaurants, which wasn't something I could do. There was a very high chance I would drop something, especially when we had to carry trays how we were told to carry them. I also would have to interact with customers, and we were told to smile at them and be polite. I am generally a polite person, but I do accidentally offend people or appear impolite without realising it. Usually I wouldn't be able to get out of having to do these things, but I would find a way of still not doing them - even though I had been sent to do them.

My main way was to be incredibly helpful. I would listen out for any time someone wanted help with something not customer-related, and I would then volunteer to help. Obviously I didn't volunteer for things that would make me more uncomfortable than being a waiter, but some of the things I volunteered for did still make me anxious - like if I agreed to get something from somewhere, I would usually get lost, I wouldn't have planned what I was going to say to whomever I was meeting to collect what I was picking up; I didn't know how the conversation was going to go, and I would often struggle to find my way back to the restaurant. But I would be going through most of this alone, and if I was lost for a while, it meant I had taken more of my shift up, all the while leaving less time for someone to ask me to work as a waiter.

Once, the changes got too much for me, so I walked out. This was in the days before everybody had mobile phones, and I didn't have a landline, so the only way to contact me was to visit me. Luckily for me, my doorbell didn't work, so even visiting me didn't guarantee that you would actually manage to get hold of me. But when I walked out, I had a manager who seemed to actually be bothered by this. He didn't have any reason to be - there were always plenty of people who wanted jobs at Butlin's who could have replaced me - but he came to my studio flat and shouted outside the building to get my attention. Eventually, after a couple of weeks of him coming to my flat, I agreed to go back into work.

I didn't have any income for these couple of weeks, and it didn't cross my mind that this was an issue. When I started working at Butlin's, I was living in Littlehampton still and would cycle eight miles to work and eight miles home every day. After a year or so, I had moved to a studio flat in Bognor, within walking distance of Butlin's. During the winter when Butlin's was only open from Friday through to Monday, my take home pay per week was less than my rent. I had tried to get council tax benefit because I couldn't afford to pay it. I was told by the local council that I should be eligible, given my circumstances, for exemption, as I wasn't even earning enough to cover my rent. It turned out that I couldn't get council tax benefit, probably because I was only 18 at the time, and I had to pay back the council tax I hadn't paid - even though I'd been advised not to do so by the council. I had this taken from my weekly pay, so I had even less to use to cover my rent.

During the winter season, I didn't put any money in the electric meter, which took pound coins, and each week I paid £45 to my landlord; my rent was £48 per week. I didn't buy food - I used to eat at work on Friday afternoon, Saturday, Sunday and Monday morning and then wouldn't eat again until the next Friday. I would sit at home in my studio flat with no heating or electric, and access to just cold water all week. I didn't mind this, though. I liked my own company, and didn't think about being hungry or anything during the week. So, making myself unemployed initially didn't bother me. I got some cans of baked beans to eat cold and didn't think much about the future.

I had never heard about signing on and claiming benefits instead of working, so I didn't think of going to the job centre to sign on. I had been in the job centre before, but thought it was where you went to get a job; I didn't know it was also where you went to claim unemployment benefits. For the two weeks I was unemployed, I didn't try to get another job, I didn't have any thoughts about doing something different. I think my plan was just to do nothing which - writing it now - sounds like a really stupid plan. I should have been thinking about getting another job. I was content with sitting at home, barely eating, having no heating or electric, and at the end of the first week when my next rent was due not having the money to pay the landlord, and again at the end of the second week. I assumed that would happen for a while, and then I would move to the woods and live there. I didn't have any problem with where my life was going, or how this may sound to other people. The thought of having nothing and ending up living alone in the woods was fine with me. I knew places in the woods I could go to keep dry, and knew I had the skills to keep myself warm. I was also confident about finding enough food and water, and I didn't feel any attachment to people. In fact, I liked the thought of being away from people and perhaps almost never seeing people again - just being at one with nature.

After about two weeks of visiting me, my old Butlin's manager talked me into coming back. I said what needed to change, which included demoting me from a section leader, and promoting someone I felt deserved to be section leader into that position, and letting me just get on with my work in the pot wash. A year or so later, I left Butlin's again, because they closed down to make some modifications to the camp. I was kept on but had to do chalet cleaning during this time. I worked for one day and decided I couldn't hack it. I quit straight away and got another job, but the same manager encouraged me to come back again, so I returned part-time, although I was doing almost full-time hours. He agreed to me being paid the highest non-manager pay it was possible to be paid.

But, still, I only stayed part-time for a few months, as that manager moved to a different position and some of the new senior staff didn't like the fact that staff would come to me for advice; they stopped my pay, and tried to encourage me to quit the job. How pay was calculated was that we had a time sheet with our expected work hours, then, by the end of the week, this would be messy with amendments showing our actual work hours. A new sheet was written showing the actual hours we worked, and this new clean sheet was sent to payroll who worked out our pay and paid us. The new senior staff didn't add me to the clean timesheet, which meant I wasn't getting paid. Initially, I thought it was an error, then I realised it wasn't - they were trying to encourage me to leave.

Because they wanted me to leave I decided to stay, and continued to work around 39 hours per week at Butlin's. I tried to see if I could do something about the issue but it was difficult to prove what they were doing. I could prove I wasn't being paid, but I couldn't prove I had definitely done the work each week, and I had a full-time job at this point, so I had no motivation to be fighting them and making myself feel uncomfortable by having to interact and argue with people. Money isn't the most important thing to me, so although I was doing the job mainly because I wanted the income, I felt I could try to fight them through the HR department and talking with the people in payroll - although at 19 years old, at that time, I had no idea how to do that and how to stand up against adults and argue my case and what that would all entail. I was happier sticking to what I knew: I would leave on my terms when I was ready, and not because they pushed me out. So this is what I did.

At the height of the summer period, I ended a shift by cleaning the pot wash machine thoroughly - taking it to pieces to clean each and every part of it. This machine was reasonably new, and I was the only member of staff present and interested for the whole time they fitted it, so I knew how to take the whole thing apart to clean it. Once I cleaned it, I left it in neat piles on the floor ready to be reassembled, but it turned out that no-one knew how to put it back together, and I didn't go back. It turned out that they had to call the manufacturers to reassemble it, but that took time, so in the meantime they had to wash everything by hand during one of the busiest times of the year.

When I started working at Butlin's, I quickly found myself invited out to have drinks after my shifts. I had drunk some alcohol through my childhood, like being given cider to try, but it wasn't something I gave any thought to. I had also accidentally got drunk at school on wine once when we had an art exhibition, at which the teachers told us students to hand out glasses of wine to parents and guests during the exhibition. They told us we could have a glass of wine or two as well... I had a glass or two, or maybe a few more than that, as I didn't realise that they would make me feel funny and make my co-ordination skills less than perfect. I carried a tray of the rented wine glasses upstairs to the home economics classrooms where the sinks were to clean them, and walked straight into the closed double doors to the upstairs corridor, smashing many of the glasses on the tray. I thought for some reason that the door would open away from me and that I could just push the tray on the doors, carefully nudging the doors open. This obviously isn't what happened.

But other than a couple of occasions, and this one occasion where I had definitely got drunk without realising it until it was too late, I had never drunk alcohol. Being under 18 when I started at Butlin's, the first times I was invited out, others would always buy me my drinks. I was uncomfortable being out with my colleagues; I didn't know what to talk to them about, and didn't know how to dance. I had danced occasionally with my mum and nan as a child, where they would guide me through ballroom dancing steps - and on a skiing trip to France, there was a disco where the teachers and children all danced, but I didn't know how. I remember asking my form tutor's son if he could tell me how to dance to the music playing. I explained I didn't know the dance moves to the songs. He said there weren't any dance moves, you just let yourself move to the music - so I never danced on the trip. To me, I like structure. I like understanding what I am supposed to do and how I am supposed to do it; I don't like being told to do whatever I feel like. I want clear dance moves that I can practice until I can do them well enough, and then I will join in by doing those moves. If I haven't yet learnt the moves, I won't be dancing.

But when you are out at a club with colleagues and dancing comes up, what do you do? For me, I would drink. I found as long as I had a drink in my hand which needed finishing, I could always be drinking and so not having to dance, and not having to engage in conversations with others. I also found that being the one who 'sacrificed' dancing to sit looking after the bags helped to get me off the hook. The main drink I used to have was snakebite and black. I would have up to 18 pints in a night. I definitely used to get drunk, but it took a lot to get me drunk. From my training about the effects of alcohol on young people, I now know that young people are most likely not exaggerating when they say they drink a lot and don't get drunk. The part of the brain that gets affected by alcohol isn't developed enough yet for them to feel drunk, but the scary thing is that the alcohol concentration in their blood is still increasing; they could very easily die of alcohol poisoning without realising how drunk they were. I think in the early days, this happened to me. I would drink and drink. I would occasionally be sick, and would feel a bit light-headed, but not as drunk as I would get from alcohol when I was a bit older.

As time went on, some colleague warned me that I was drinking too much and that I should stop drinking or cut down. These were people who were also out every night drinking and partying. At my worst I would work from 7am through to 11pm, then drink through to 6am socially, before sitting outside the venue and trying to sober up before starting work at 7am. I would do this about six days a week, sometimes. I didn't 'enjoy' the drink. I drank as if I was drinking water - but it was what you did. You didn't go out drinking and have water or coke; you went out drinking and people would say "what are you having?" and they meant what alcoholic drink, so you would name a drink. After a while, I stopped drinking snakebite and black and started with spirits instead. I was drinking either Jack Daniels, Southern Comfort, or Vodka, always with cola. This was mainly because I didn't need the toilet so often with these drinks - they are less liquid than drinking pints.

I only ever drank socially as that seemed what people did. It also gave me something to do. If I was drinking a drink, I didn't look so awkward and didn't tap all the time, or whistle, or copy people. I could have a glass up to my mouth and a hand on the glass. I still use this technique today, but instead of gulping drinks back, I will sip a drink as slowly as I can while I stand or sit in a corner, not engaging with anyone. People don't seem to question it as long as you have a drink in your hand, or food, so that you appear occupied.

I did find that drinking alcohol would help me reach a point where I would be more confident to do things like dance without structure, but I also found I had poorer co-ordination, so it was a fine line between getting the benefits from drinking, and tipping over into the negatives of being too drunk. Once I had been going out almost every night for many months, I started to go onto the dance floor, and after a while, I started dancing and gradually got used to dancing to different songs. I did my best to copy what others were doing. Eventually, I didn't need to drink to have confidence to dance, because I was dancing every night. It takes a lot to convince me to dance nowadays, because I don't do so often, but when I was doing it regularly I had no problem doing what I had done the previous night. This didn't stop me drinking, though, because my main reason for drinking wasn't to gain confidence - rather, it was so that I continually had something to do.

What stopped me drinking was when I went out, aged 19, with colleagues and my new girlfriend. Late at night I hugged her and told her I loved her. The next day she told me that when I'd hugged her, I crushed her and it hurt. Obviously when I was very drunk, I couldn't feel my own body very well, so didn't notice how tightly I'd hugged her. But I instantly decided that if I could hurt someone I love because of being drunk, then I didn't want to drink any more. I went through a period of having my heart racing, and shaking, as if I was having anxiety attacks and sweating - but all of this ended after a few days. I didn't drink anything for the next year, and after that, I have only ever drunk alcohol in moderation, with just a few occasions of actually getting drunk. Today, I probably have a couple of drinks once or twice per year, and some years haven't had any alcohol at all. The thought that I could do something I thought of as loving and kind, and yet could actually hurt someone because of being drunk was enough to motivate me to never want to habitually drink like that again. Even if I do drink on an evening out I am always mindful of that experience.

I would never have called myself an alcoholic, though I know some colleagues of mine at the time said I was one, but I definitely would have said I had a drink problem. Once I stopped drinking, a few problems presented themselves. One was: what should I do now to look occupied? The other was people trying to push me into having a drink. My solution was to have cola in a glass, just like the one the Jack Daniel's and coke used to come in. That way, people would assume I had a drink no different to normal. I also started sipping my drinks so that the glass would remain full for longer. That way, if anyone offered to get me a drink, I would say "I have got one", and would show them my glass. Usually this was enough for people to leave me alone. I didn't need alcohol to dance, and didn't need alcohol to have the same type of evening.

Key differences were that I was awake for more of the evening: I had no problem getting myself home, I wasn't sick, I didn't spend lots of money, and I didn't wake up with a hangover, or trying to remember what had happened the previous night - something I had only ever experienced once through all my time drinking heavily. I had drunk a pint of 100% proof strong vodka, gulping it back in seconds, and even now, I only remember about five minutes or so from that point. The next day I woke up at a work colleague's house; he told me I passed out as we were walking home from Butlin's. We'd both had to walk in the same direction, but my home was about three times further than where he lived. He said he picked me up and was carrying me but I was a dead weight. He rested me over a flint wall to catch his breath, but I just slid down the wall into a heap on the floor, which explained the scratches to my face I had sustained. Then, the police drove past and pulled over. They decided to help.

My colleague said he lived just around the corner; he thought that maybe I should stay there and sleep it off where he could keep an eye on me. They agreed and put me in the back of their police car. Apparently, when we arrived at our destination I hooked my legs under the front seat and refused to be moved; they had some difficulty getting me out of the car and into the flat. Eventually they managed it. Then, the next day, I woke up unable to recall any of this. I had a horrible hangover, and I had to work all day - that was a really difficult and long day's work.

I used to also make concoctions, mixing different drinks - like pernod with vodka, Jack Daniel's and Southern Comfort - and I would buy cheap cider and distil it by boiling off the alcohol into another saucepan. I would take a three or four litre bottle of cider, and turn it into a small amount of alcohol which I would add to a bottle of drink, to create a stronger, more alcoholic drink for cheaper. I usually did this because it was something to talk about that wasn't football - or something equally as boring to me. If I said to people, "Why don't we mix drinks? Why don't you try this? Look, I've distilled this cider and made this drink," then people would engage in that topic of conversation. I didn't meet people who wanted to talk about hypnosis, or about psychology or philosophy, and I didn't want to talk about the boring things they did, but I wanted to appear normal and to try to fit in. The alternative was to do nothing every night, to always say no to every invitation to go out, and to have people think I'm odd. Nowadays, I am happy to have people think I'm odd - I am happy to just be me - but back then, I thought the right thing to do was to fit in, and at least to try to behave as people wanted me to behave.

Sometimes, on nights out, I would run into difficulties because of having Asperger's. An example is that I feel a compulsion to crush boxes in specific ways: I like to crush small cigarette packs by applying weight to them with my hand, and gradually increasing that weight until the corners give way. I did this on a night out with a cigarette box that was on the table. I was in my own little world when I saw the box and decided to do this, I didn't think about whether the box had cigarettes in or not. It turned out that it did, and the owner wasn't happy. He jumped up aggressively pushing his chair back with his legs, shouting and swearing at me. I remember looking up at him, unsure as to why he was angry, then one of the girls at the table, sat beside him, stood up and got in front of the aggressive man and told him to calm down and sit down. She told him I was weird and would do things like that. He started to calm down a little as he picked up the cigarette packet and looked inside noticing the cigarettes were a bit crushed, but not really damaged.

I have a thing about pressure, see. Like when I stick a knife through the lid of a microwave meal, I like to hold the knife with my left hand, with the point of the blade resting on the top of the plastic, then rest the palm of my right hand on top of the knife and gently push to the point at which the knife just about breaks through the lid.

During my time at Butlin's, I struggled with people's attitudes and their disdain for following rules. To me, rules are helpful. They let me know what I am supposed to be doing from moment to moment. I like following rules or processes, especially when there are very good logical reasons to do so. I was put in charge of health and safety in the venue I worked in. It used to confuse me when people would decide not to exhibit common sense safety behaviours, like wearing safety equipment when using hazardous chemicals. Back then, I had very little empathy for people. If someone did something potentially hazardous and they had been warned or advised against what they were doing, or had been given the relevant safety equipment and they chose not to use it, my view was that they were accepting the consequences of their actions if anything happened.

I had an experience where a manager of mine was about to clean the walls of the pot wash. She had a cleaning chemical, highly concentrated, in an ice cream tub and was going to slosh it over the wall and then scrub it. I told her to wear goggles, as that was the recommendation when using the chemical. She refused saying, she wasn't going to look stupid by wearing goggles. I said, if she didn't wear them, she may get the chemical into her eyes and it could burn. She ignored me and threw the chemical at the wall. It duly hit the wall and splashed back in her eyes. She started to scream in pain because it was stinging her eyes. I carried on working doing my usual pot washing job, paying no attention to her. As far as I was concerned, she knew the consequences of her actions and, by choosing the actions, she was obviously accepting the consequences that could occur. Nowadays, although my thinking is exactly the same, I have had enough people telling me that the 'right thing to do' is to pretend you care and to help the person, so I would now help. I wouldn't have any sympathy for the person, but I would do what others say is the correct response.

There was a member of staff who came into the pot wash and was acting all cocky. He grabbed hold of the conveyor belt whilst it was moving. I had just put some bits on it and was walking to the other end to take them off the conveyor belt. I told the lad to stop messing around with the machine, I told him it was dangerous, that there was almost boiling hot water, and that if he got caught on the conveyor belt whilst messing around and got pulled into it, he would have chemicals sprayed over him and very hot water. He continued to pull on the conveyor belt, trying to stop it, and joking that he was strong enough to be able to stop it. Then, the ring on one of his fingers got caught on one of the hooks of the conveyor belt - he started to get pulled into the machine. He tried reaching up with his other hand to the stop button, but he couldn't reach. He started screaming for help. I was at the other end of the machine, waiting for the clean items to come out. Then, someone who had heard him screaming came in to the pot wash and hit the emergency stop button, by the door to the restaurant, so the lad didn't get dragged all the way into the machine. I didn't think to stop the machine - because he had decided he didn't mind going into the machine. If he did mind, he wouldn't have carried on doing his behaviour - that would be illogical.

Again, I have since been told that the correct thing to do would have been to stop the machine so that the person didn't get hurt. I can understand this if an accident had happened, like if someone was working away loading the machine, and perhaps their watch got caught on it - but someone choosing to do what they did was also choosing the potential consequences that went with it. If a similar thing happened, I would stop the machine now, but I would have no sympathy for the person; I have just learnt from those who are open and honest with me about my perceptions of things, and what the correct thing to do is. In future roles, like as a carer, my role has included doing certain behaviours, so if a teenager I was caring for refused to wear goggles and so got a chemical in their eyes, my job as a care worker would be to ensure the care of that person - so I would do what the relevant response was: getting an ambulance, or getting water and helping them wash their eyes out. I wouldn't feel anything like concern for them; I wouldn't act shocked or panic; I would just matter-of-factly and calmly carry out the process I am supposed to carry out.

Butlin's was where I met the person who was to become my first wife. She is the one whom I hugged and crushed - the incident that led to me giving up drinking alcohol. Back then, I was still only young. I was 19 when I met her, and I wasn't very good with knowing how to behave emotionally. We were together for four years, and married briefly at the end of that period. I loved her and wanted the relationship to work, but I definitely didn't have the skills to be the person I needed to be in the relationship. Even when it ended, I reacted with what was my usual non-emotional, matter-of-fact response. I walked away. I didn't get upset. I looked at the situation logically; if she didn't want to be with me, and had decided that, then, as her happiness was important to me, then that was the outcome that would happen and I would move on with my life.

My best friend, whom I also met at Butlin's, said I needed to 'let out my feelings'; I kept trying to explain I don't feel anything. I wasn't saying that to be cold or appear tough in some way, I genuinely didn't feel anything. I had moved on. He said I needed to get angry - I needed to get drunk. I disagreed with both of these statements. I did get angry with her, but it wasn't over the break-up; it was due to her lying about something. It was a petty and unimportant lie, but to me honesty is important. I can accept people lying, because I know that people lie for different reasons, including to protect the feelings of others. But, to accept lying, I have to be able to see a logical argument as to why the person felt lying was the best course of action. That doesn't mean I agree with their lie, it just means I understand their decision to lie. Because of this, often, small lies have more of an impact on me than big lies, because big lies usually have a reason. Given the circumstances of us no longer being together and her knowing what I was like as a person, I saw no reason for the lie, and so got angry. My best friend and my brother were present to calm me down in that moment.

Because my mentality was that, once my wife and I separated, I moved on, it only took a few months before I was in another relationship. I didn't seek the relationship out, but I didn't get plagued with thoughts of "it's too soon", or any of these feelings I hear others talk about. If I met someone and thought I would like to have a relationship with them, I was going to just say it, which is what I did. I let the person know I wanted to go out with her, and eventually, she agreed to go out with me. I don't think I was very good 'boyfriend material' back then. I didn't feel I was affectionate or attentive enough in my previous relationship, and I hadn't learnt those skills in time for this relationship either. Back then, my level of experiencing and understanding emotions was very low. I would watch horror films all the time because some would have the power to make me jump, which would get a response out of me. But the girl I met stuck by me, despite me struggling to show attentiveness, emotional understanding and responsiveness; as time passed, I reached a point when I knew something had shifted, because I suddenly struggled to watch horror films. I started to find them too gory. I started to cringe at certain films and find them too uncomfortable to watch. This girl has so far stood by me for 15 years, and has gone on to become my wife. She has already taught me so much and continues to do so, and I have been learning from my mistakes. A good example is when I worked in a job, and a year into that job I was involved in an accident and ended up in hospital. My wife came to visit me in hospital, and while she was there, my work colleagues turned up to visit. My wife introduced herself, and they told her they didn't know I was in a relationship with anyone. She wasn't happy that I had worked with a team of staff members for a year and had never mentioned her. My perspective was that it had never come up in conversation. I couldn't understand why it would, or why they would be interested in any way by my personal life. I had talked to them a lot about hypnosis, but not about who I was going out with. Since this event, I have always made sure people know I am married and - even though I don't understand why I should do it - I mention my wife.

As I have mentioned before, it didn't cross my mind to keep in contact with friends from school. I have never set out to make friends. If I ended up with a friend, then it somehow just happened that way. With my best friend, I didn't set out for us to be friends, and he didn't set out to be friends with me initially. He worked mainly in the burger bar, a place where the manager was fiddling the till. The manager boasted to me that he was making a fortune; he was running £2.80 meals through the till as 80p drinks, so that every five meals put the till £10 up, and as soon as there was £10 extra in the till, he removed it. He said he didn't do it with all customers, but with about 20-30 customers per day. He said management were too stupid to catch him, so I told management what he was doing and how to catch him and got him sacked. A few days later, I was in his flat. He was making me a cup of tea and was angry at being sacked, saying he thought he knew who'd got him in trouble, and asking if I had any idea who it was. I told him I knew who it was, and that it was me. He stopped making me a cup of tea and kicked me out. I didn't realise until a few years later, when a lad tried to beat me up and I couldn't understand why, that he wasn't the only one doing this; many other staff were as well and all those who got caught got the sack. Obviously I had revealed I was the reason they lost their jobs.

My best friend used to come into the pot wash to get cleaning items, or other things, depending on where he was working that day. Like with everyone else, I didn't talk to him. I just watched him walk in, get what he needed, and then walk out. He described me as being weird and intimidating. He was only 14 at the time, I was 19. The girl I was going out with (my first wife) was far more chatty, sociable and friendly than I, and she got on well with him. I think she thought we would get on if I would actually talk to him, rather than glare at him. One day, somehow, we got into a conversation about how I had a large collection of videos, including horror videos, TV series videos and science fiction videos. Unlike most people I knew at Butlin's, this lad seemed to be interested in some of what I was interested in. Soon after first talking with him, I found out from my girlfriend that he needed a place to stay, so I recommended that he stayed with us. We only lived in a studio flat, but he could sleep on the floor, and after a short while, we bought a large 3-seater blow-up sofa for him to sleep on.

I had never heard of social services at this point, and when they heard a 14-year-old boy was living with a 19-year-old lad and his 17-year-old girlfriend, they felt this was inappropriate. I couldn't understand why at the time. We were both well behaved - we didn't go out getting drunk or anything - and we both had full-time jobs. All we were doing was trying to help a teenager who needed somewhere to stay. Now, almost 20 years later, we are still best friends and still keep in touch. He always called me Spock, and when I told him I had been diagnosed with Asperger's he was very apologetic, saying he didn't mean any offence by calling me Spock for all those years, and had he known I was the way I am because I had Asperger's, he never would have called me that. He would often refer to me as 'his Vulcan friend' and I used to say he was like Captain Kirk. He was totally illogical and ruled by emotions, whereas I was rational and logical, and struggled to access any emotion.

Calling me Spock was a compliment. For years, I had looked up to Spock as someone who had some emotions and would get confused when they appeared - he would try to intellectualise the experience to understand the emotion, but usually his life was ruled by logic and reason and rationality. He also faced some discrimination for being different, but most of those who made comments were also people who liked and cared for him; they just thought he was a bit weird. He also managed to make friends with Captain Kirk, despite being almost polar opposites. This mirrored our relationship. Another Star Trek character I had looked up to was Data from The Next Generation. He was like

Spock, but without any initial emotional programming. Through the course of the series he gradually learnt how he was supposed to respond in different situations, and started having emotional experiences he at first didn't realise or understand were emotional 'human' experiences; gradually, he evolved, developed and learnt.

I have mentioned before about leaving Butlin's after one day of cleaning chalets. I knew there was no way I could handle that experience for a second day, so I went to the job centre and found a job. Back in 1998, it was so much easier to find a job than it is today. Progress seems to be about making things more difficult, rather than what I think progress should be - making things easier. I walked into the job centre and all around the walls were cards with jobs on. So I started at one end, and worked my way round the walls looking at the different jobs, trying to find something I thought I could do. I didn't have many qualifications and my work experience was working in Butlin's pot wash. I doubted that I would find a similar pot wash job, but I thought that I would find something that I was able to do.

By being able to look at all the jobs, rather than having to try to search like you have to do now, I was able to find a job I thought I could do - even though I had never tried it before. The job was working for a company that had two homes for people with mental health problems. I saw that the job didn't require any previous experience or qualifications, and I thought I would find it interesting learning about mental health challenges like schizophrenia, manic depression, severe obsessive compulsive disorder, and autism. I had been interested in psychology due to my interest in hypnosis (my girlfriend at the time was scared by the thought of me doing hypnosis, so I barely pursued that interest while we were together), and this job would allow me to pursue my interests. I got the job to start straightaway, so I didn't go into Butlin's the next day - instead, I went into my new workplace. I went back to Butlin's when it reopened, but only as additional work.

## Magic of an unorthodox mind

Working in a care home for adults with mental health difficulties was totally different to working in a holiday camp. The first thing I liked was working in a small team. In one home I worked in, there were nine residents and one member of staff on shift, and the other home had about fifteen residents and two members of staff on shift. The managers worked about 9-5 and would spend most of their time in the larger home, just popping into the smaller home occasionally through the day to see how things were going. When I first started, I worked in the larger home with a more experienced member of staff. The shifts were either 8am to 2pm or 2pm to 8pm, and then once per week I slept in on my own from 8pm to 8am. The shift pattern was a week of early shifts followed by a week of late shifts. I used to like the late shifts, because the managers would be gone by about 5pm so there would just be myself, another member of staff and the residents present.

We did all the chores, issuing medication and looking after the residents. There were no staff coming in to cook or clean. I liked this, because it meant I could keep occupied. On the morning shift, the residents needed waking up, medication and breakfast before about

9:30am, then we had to clear away after breakfast and do the washing up. Then, we had to clean the house, vacuum round, change bedding, do laundry, prepare lunch and give out lunchtime medication. After lunch, we had to spend time with residents and support them with certain things. Each member of staff had certain residents they were responsible for supporting and doing the care plan for, so we had to ensure the care plan was suitable, up-to-date, and being followed.

In the afternoon, we would come on shift and have to prepare tea and coffee, then clear that away, then cook dinner, which could often take a couple of hours, then serve dinner and give out medication, then clear away and wash up after dinner. Finally, we'd prepare evening drinks for the residents before the shift ended. The night shift was just offering residents drinks and a snack in the evening, giving medication before bed, helping anyone get ready for bed who needed it, and making sure all residents were in the home and alright before the end of the night. We also had to be available if anyone needed support during the night.

There were other tasks that came up from time to time, like having to sort out shopping when it arrived, checking stock, health and safety checks and fire alarm checks, but the days were generally very structured with what needed to be done and when. I liked this structure. As part of the job, we were given mental health training. Doing this job was the first time I experienced helping people, but I sometimes got in trouble for helping. I was told that my job was to care for the residents, not to help them; but I felt if I could help then I would. There was a resident who was in his early twenties and had severe obsessive compulsive disorder (OCD) around cleanliness.

The ironic thing was that he created a dirtier environment because of his OCD, which was upsetting other residents, some of whom had started bullying him because of it. For example, he would go to the toilet, but because he was scared of germs and dirt he wouldn't touch himself, so he would urinate all over the toilet seat and floor.

One day, I gave him a box of sterile latex gloves and told him that they were clean - I told him he could put them on whenever he needed to clean something or touch something that was dirty, and then he could throw them away afterwards. I showed him how to take them off without touching the outside of the gloves with either hand. He started using the gloves, which led to him cleaning up after himself, and not leaving mess (for example, in the toilet). This led to the bullying stopping and he was calmer, happier and more relaxed. My employers told me off for helping him, telling me that this wasn't my job; it was the job of his psychiatrist. His social worker praised me personally saying, in all the years he had been in care (since his youth), no-one had helped him, and this was the first time he seemed happy and wanted to be in a placement.

A skill I think many people with Asperger's have is being able to notice patterns and find simple answers. This was something I began to notice as a real asset when working in care. Many people also have this thought that people with Asperger's don't have feelings. In fact, we do. Feelings are something I find very difficult to describe. I find when I start describing how I feel, I end up saying things that sound contradictory. For example, I want everyone to be happy and have the best opportunities in life, but I don't feel like I generally care about people as individuals. I like doing care work because it allows me to learn about subjects I am interested in, and I like solving problems; people have problems, and problems are just patterns to be solved.

Working in the mental health homes, I met many residents whose stories other staff found distressing. I could understand that it probably wasn't pleasant for those people to go through the experiences they'd had, but I didn't take on any of the feelings myself - because it wasn't me who'd had those experiences. To me, I think this is a real strength that people with Asperger's have; it makes us good psychological therapists. Many people with Asperger's are detached from the emotional content of the stories of others, which is something most therapists struggle with and have to learn, in order to be able to help people without being clouded by emotions, or the story of the client or patient.

Working in care homes involves a lot of writing. Unfortunately, this means I had pens on me far more often than in my previous work - and these pens usually had clickable, retractable nibs - so I would click the pen for hours at a time. Many staff would eventually comment about how annoyed they were getting with me clicking the pens. I tried to stop clicking, but as they were always in the office, somehow a pen would always end up in my hand and I would be clicking it repeatedly, without noticing that I was doing so.

After a few years of working in mental health, I ended up working in children's homes with teenagers who exhibited challenging behaviour. The mental health company I worked for was making some changes and I wasn't comfortable with those changes, so I looked for a different job. I didn't have any expectations about the children's home job; I just knew I needed to get out of the previous job before the changes came in. I left the mental health job on the Friday before the changes, and started the new job on the Monday. I wasn't really prepared for what the new job was going to entail. I was told that when I arrived on my first day, I needed to walk around the back of the house and enter through the back door. When I arrived, I did so; a member of staff greeted me and said he would show me through to the office. As we were walking through the kitchen/dining room, one of the teenagers grabbed me by my collar with both hands, pinned me to the wooden post between the kitchen and the dining room, got his face almost nose to nose with me and shouted, "Who the fuck are you, and what are you doing in my house?!"

At this moment, I remember wondering whether I had made the right decision changing jobs. I had residents in my last workplace become aggressive at times, but not specifically at me, in this way. I didn't feel scared or intimidated, but I wasn't particularly happy with someone being in my personal space and touching me like that. I told him who I was and that I had just started working there; the member of staff I was with told him to let go of me. He let go, and we went to walk out of the kitchen. As we walked into the corridor there was commotion in the living room. It sounded like someone was throwing and smashing things. The boy in the living room was also shouting and swearing aggressively. We were heading out of the kitchen, turning left in the corridor, where the living room door was in the corner on the right. Two staff members appeared from the corridor to the left, running into the lounge. As myself

173

and the man I was with walked past the lounge, I could see a teenage boy being restrained on the floor. This was definitely a different pace to my last job.

Over the five years working in residential children's homes, I had been involved in many violent and life threatening situations. I had been attacked with knives, broken glass, baseball bats; I'd been punched, kicked, bitten, headbutted, and much more. Violence was almost a daily occurrence. The staff turnover was very high. I trained up to teach the restraint training and behaviour management course which staff had to do when they started working in the children's homes. Of ten staff I would teach, three would be left six months later, and only one would be left a year later. I worked with teenagers with a wide range of different problems; some had attention deficit hyperactivity disorder (ADHD), or oppositional defiance disorder (ODD), others had Asperger's, and some had lower functioning autism. Some had been through difficult childhoods, experiencing sexual or physical abuse or neglect, or emotional abuse. Many experienced post-traumatic stress disorder (PTSD) and had anxiety and anger problems - and many used drugs and alcohol regularly. The teenagers were there for all different reasons. Some had been abusers themselves, and others had been abused; some were taken from their families for their own safety, while others had families who didn't want them anymore.

Many staff who started working in the children's homes were there because they cared and wanted to make a difference, but many aspects of the job were just too much for them to handle. If a teenager who was a paedophile was talking graphically in front of staff about how they had raped babies, for example, some staff would find it difficult to keep calm, to maintain emotional neutrality, and to treat that young person as non-judgementally as the others. Other staff found the violence too much to handle when they were going in to work and on each shift they'd be physically assaulted, and some staff would get upset with stories the children would tell about their past, like if a child mentioned about their mum letting men into their bedroom every night whom they had to fight, and that they didn't like these fights because the men always hurt them.

Because I didn't take on the emotions of others in these situations, I was able to remain calm and clear-headed. I could think rationally to handle situations. To me, working in residential childcare was an opportunity to study human behaviour and how people interact with each other. I was able to learn about people, and I was sent on many training courses about child and teen development - about drug and alcohol use, about all sorts of topics related to children and young people. I definitely thought I was good at the job. I was able to remain emotionally detached. I worked well in very small teams (there were normally only two staff on shift, sometimes three, with two staff sleeping in), and I was good at problem-solving and finding novel solutions. I would come up with ideas others wouldn't think of.

An example of helping a child with a novel solution - which my employers felt was just covering over the problem, whereas I felt I was making a start at helping a child feel better - was a child who had been abused in a bathroom at a much younger age. This had led to them being unwilling to have a bath or shower in the bathroom, and getting them to bathe was a battle. They were thus bullied due to being smelly. I found out they liked the idea of trying swimming, so I took them to the swimming pool. They were happy to use the showers in a swimming pool, because the showers in the pool aren't in a location that resembles a bathroom. Regularly swimming and showering meant they were calmer and more relaxed in the home, and they were no longer being bullied because of being smelly. So this, on its own, didn't necessarily help them fully move on, but it was a step in the right direction - something to build on. As systemic therapists would think, changing part of the pattern will have an effect on the whole pattern; it is just about trying to make the smallest change in the right direction to start the process off.

I'll now give two examples of handling potentially violent situations with novel solutions. Firstly, a teenager went to attack me in the dining room of a children's home. I saw a cricket bat leaning against the wall in the corner of the room beside me, so I picked up the bat and gave it to the teenager and said, "Here, why don't you have this?" I did this for a very good reason, even if it sounds illogical on the surface. Once people are given a weapon to use, they usually want to use it. I don't really want to be hit with a bat, but without the bat, I didn't know if he was likely to grab me and pin me to a wall, or grab me and throw me to the floor, or headbutt me, or punch me with his left or right hand, or elbow me, or knee me, or kick me, or scratch me, or bite me, or do any other thing he could think of. By giving him a bat, though, I was reasonably sure he was going to take it with two hands and try to swing it at me to hit me. I was stood close to him - close enough to hand him the bat - so I was too close for him to swing it at me successfully. We had a dining room table beside us, and a wall on the other side of us, and I had a wall and door to the kitchen right behind me. The door from the dining room out into the corridor was about four metres behind the teenager. My aim was to make myself safer and to resolve the situation, ideally removing myself, as he was being aggressive towards me at that time. By giving him the bat, I made his behaviour more predictable. What ended up happening was that he put the bat down, told me I was crazy and walked away.

The other example was a teenager with razorblades threatening to 'cut up' anyone who went in the lounge. As staff, we had to do something, so I stepped into the lounge and sat on the sofa. As I walked in to the lounge, I said: "If you decide to try to cut me up that will be up to you, but I would rather sit here and find out if there is any way I can help you." He then spoke to me for a while, before saying "I suppose you'll be wanting these now" and giving me the razorblades. Again, this may sound like I was doing something which could put me at more risk, but the sofa was beside the lounge door, so I was still by the door. He was sat across the other side of the room, about six or eight metres away. If he had jumped up to go for me, I would have made it the couple of steps out of the door and had the door shut behind me faster than he would have made it across the room to me. There were other staff just outside the door who were able to help if needed, and if things had escalated - or we hadn't been able to safely get the razorblades from the teen - we would have called the police; as with all childcare work like this, though, the whole aim was to try not to have to call the police, because we didn't want to criminalise children.

Sometimes I would get in trouble doing childcare, because there were a lot of meetings, and so I started having a lot of contact with people where we were just sat around. When I am doing something practical, or when I see people for very short amounts of time, I can put effort in to being as still and quiet as possible; but when I am in a situation long enough for my mind to start wandering, I don't notice that I start doing things unless people point it out to me. In a meeting with staff and managers one of the managers was called away to take a phone call. While the manager was out of the room, everyone was sitting quietly and - without noticing, because we weren't doing anything and there was nothing specific for me to focus on - my mind started to wander. I started to whistle and make different noises. The manager left in the room told me to stop, and that was when I noticed I had been doing something. I asked "Stop what?" He told me to stop whistling, so as far as I am aware, I didn't whistle for the rest of the meeting. I focused on different things around the room to stop myself from drifting into my mind. A couple of days later, the manager met with me to discipline me for my actions which he had taken offence to. He told me I was rude - I'd whistled in a meeting, and when he told me to stop, I didn't even apologise for my whistling. I didn't know I was supposed to apologise; I wasn't asked to apologise, I was asked to stop whistling. He also said that I was rude by answering him back in the meeting when I asked him "Stop what?" I explained to the manager I do this sometimes: I start whistling and I don't know why, and I don't even notice I am doing it. The manager told me not to let it happen again.

I was also threatened with disciplinary action, and was told I could even get the sack if I didn't start saying good morning and goodbye to people. A manager told me that some of the staff had complained about how I'd arrive on shift without saying good morning or goodbye to them when they left work or I went home. These things just don't cross my mind. I had never meant to be rude, or for anyone to be upset by my behaviour. I was always polite, and I didn't swear; it just didn't cross my mind to say good morning or goodbye to people. I was picked up on this a few times over the years. Each time I would have to spend my whole journey to work reminding myself to greet people, and during the morning handover with the staff coming on shift, instead of focusing on what I was supposed to be remembering - to tell the staff about what had happened during our shift and any important information they should be aware of - I was sitting there reminding myself to say goodbye when I left at the end of the handover.

After working in residential childcare, I started offering support to parents and families. The idea with parenting support was to support mums and dads in finding what would work for them to help their child behave. I was supporting parents of children who were either young offenders or committing anti-social behaviour and, instead of working with the children to get the children to change their behaviour, I was working with the parents to get them to change. The idea was that it is easier to have the person who is motivated to want change to happen to make a change, than to try to force someone who doesn't realise there is a problem to change. When I started doing this work, my manager - very early on in our relationship - said she thought I had

Asperger's and so she was going to treat me as if I did. This was a good thing, and generally helped me to get on well at this role. I used to walk to all my home visits, about 45 miles per week. I spent a lot of time alone, and a lot of time in nature as I walked from visit to visit. The area I covered was largely rural.

I didn't often see colleagues, and my manager said she trusted me and left me to get on with my work, just checking in with me from time to time. This all worked very well for me. I liked being alone and I liked being out in nature. I was able to apply my knowledge of managing challenging children and teens to helping parents with their teens, and I was able to apply my knowledge and therapeutic experience. My manager encouraged me to use and share my skills. I was very honest with my manager about myself. By this point in my life, I had felt discriminated against in previous roles; this time, I thought maybe if I was just open and honest and blunt about what I am like, then if something was a problem, it could be worked on or addressed. I had started to become more mindful of who I am and how I am different to others around me. Some of my colleagues in children's homes used to say I was similar to some of the children and teens, and I used to think to myself that I was similar to them too, but I didn't say anything. In one role, I had even approached a union about discrimination I felt I was receiving. They told me I was being discriminated against, but I was a 'white, male of working age without any disabilities', so there was nothing they could help me with. They advised I could either leave my job or 'be a thorn in their side and stay until I decided to leave', so I stayed until I decided to leave. I also didn't feel the union was that helpful, so I left the union as well.

I still hadn't reached a point of thinking about seeking a diagnosis for Asperger's, I hadn't looked in detail about whether it could be Asperger's I had. I thought it might be, but I didn't want to jump to that answer having never undertaken any tests. I was aware that people often self-diagnose when actually they don't show some key sign of the condition they diagnose themselves with. Like people saying they are OCD when they just like things neat and tidy. Someone with OCD would, in fact, be experiencing extreme anxiety and most likely panic attacks at the smallest thing being out of place. Their lives would likely be ruled by the OCD, rather than leading a life where you just choose for things to be tidy - or where mess annoys you. I didn't want to be like this, where I said I had something I hadn't yet been tested for, and I was reluctant to get tested, as I didn't see the benefit of a label. I was aware of too many people who had become the label, rather than the label being helpful to gain access to support or services.

I didn't really have relationships with colleagues when doing this work. I had a couple of colleagues who sat next to me when we were in the office, and I got on with my immediate team. The topic came up one day about leaving the role, and I said if I decided to leave the role, I would just leave there and then. He asked whether I would say goodbye or anything; I looked at him confused and told him I wouldn't: why would I do that? I would have left. He told me he was hurt by this, and if I ever left, I had to promise I would say goodbye - even if it was calling him up and letting him know I wouldn't be coming in anymore. I asked him why. I said I couldn't understand what that would achieve. He said he was a friend and that was what friends should do. He cared about me and would want to know I was well, and what I was doing. I told him I was still very unlikely to let him know. Another colleague asked me "Whenever I see you, you never talk to me. Why is that?" I told her it was because she only talked about boring things. I don't remember her reply, but we continued not talking to each other.

I also had incidents where people would borrow my pens and not return them, or would use my pens at my desk and lose the lid. Even though it sounds stupid as I write this, I wouldn't give up until I had found where my pen had gone and got it back, or found my lost lid. With one psychologist, I chased them for some days. They unfortunately couldn't find the lid for my biro, so they gave me a replacement.

One of the biggest issues I have had has been where I work when I'm in an office. In children's homes and other care homes, there was some office work, but it was usually just one member of staff in an office at a time working at the one desk in that office. When I stopped working in children's homes, I was looking at other work. I was applying for a wide range of different jobs, because I didn't know what would be a good job to do. I tried working in a sales shop, but wasn't comfortable with anything about the job; I didn't like how many customers there were, how the seating was arranged, the fact that so much had to be done on computers. I tried telesales, and - as soon as I walked into the room and saw dense rows of people on telephones in front of computer screens, so exposed, and all so noisy - I walked out of that. I even had a job created for me by a company who were keen to have me work for them, but I couldn't use the phone in front of people like I was expected to do, the desk I had to sit at was too exposed, and the environment was too noisy, and I had issues with the long journey to work.

The first desk I had doing parenting and family work was in a corner, with a high board blocking the view between my desk and the desk opposite. I was also beside a window, so I could gaze out the window as well if I needed to take a moment to drift off and find some peace and calm. I also had an area to go to that was like a conservatory, with benches surrounded by tall plants and indoor trees so that each section of benches felt secluded. I was able to grab a cup of water and sit there when I needed to take time out. Then, my desk was moved to another room in the same building - a smaller room with just a few desks. This room had no windows, which was fine; I was again in the corner with a wall in front of and beside me. I could absorb myself in the plain walls. I sometimes had difficulty in this room cancelling out the person next to me when he was on the phone, but frequently I could find myself in the room working alone. I then did a different role that had a desk in a different building, where I was in a corner again with high screens blocking me off from the desks around me and a window beside me. I never had anything on the screens. By having them just plain blue, I was able to focus on the plain colour to shut out distractions. By slumping in my chair a little, I was able to look at the screens and not see all the movement of other people in the room; the screens gave me something to help me focus, and to shut out sights and sounds, so that I could work on the computer or talk on the phone.

After this desk, I was told I had to move to an open-plan section of the office. I didn't want to move, and had said I wanted to stay in the corner. I explained I would be less able to work if I was placed in this new location. This is exactly what happened: I struggled to work, I was distracted by the staff around me, there were no dividing screens, I was distracted by the movement of others around the office, and the lights above me. I found it almost impossible to use the phone now, and it was very difficult to work on the computer too. I now felt anxious almost continuously, unless I was out of the office. Although I was able to work from home, I hadn't wanted to up until this point because I liked the structure of going in to work and working at a proper desk. Now I started working at home more, to avoid the office, but this also meant not being around to support my team who were based in the office. This was one of the things that encouraged me to eventually seek diagnosis. I felt I would have had more say, if I was able to have occupational health assess my working environment and give recommendations about how my environment should be set up to get the best work out of me.

Like with my other care work, I found it useful that I wouldn't get emotionally involved with what parents and families were saying to me. I wanted the best outcomes for the families, and was able to focus on identifying the patterns of the problems that were going on, then looking at what changes needed to be made and what it would take for the family members to be in a position to make these changes. I continued to try to appear 'normal', not that such a thing really exists - the one thing everyone has in common is that we are all different. There are, however, certain behaviours that most people do, and so I tried to make sure I did these behaviours. You would think that by the time I was in my 30s - and having gotten into trouble for certain behaviours - I would be able to do those behaviours easily, even if I was doing them with conscious thought and effort, rather than instinctively. But that wasn't the case. I would see someone walking towards me and know they were going to say "Morning, how are you?" and they were going to expect me to say "I'm fine, and you?" This is a very simple exchange. I would be walking towards the person saying, "I'm fine, and you? I'm fine, and you?" over and over in my mind, then when I finally passed them and they asked how I was, I would either just nod, or at best say "I'm okay". About thirty seconds later, I would realise I didn't reciprocate and ask how they were. I obviously had no interest in how they were - because that is their business, not mine - but it was what people seemed to do.

This type of communication was also an issue in my role as someone managing staff. All the staff I have managed over the years have been incredible people, hard-working and always going above and beyond what would be expected of them, but as I neared the end of my management roles, I was having 'who I was' pushed more noticeably into my awareness. This was making me aware of what a rubbish manager I actually was in some areas. My first senior role was at Butlin's, where I didn't mind what the staff did as long as customers weren't affected and all the work got done - and, obviously, as long as nothing they did was against any rules. But I did have a problem with people who went off sick for what I would think were not good enough reasons.

In over twenty years of working, I have missed one day of work - which wasn't my actual shift. I had agreed to do it as overtime and because I was very ill (vomiting black sick, stomach cramps and hallucinating - apparently I had tonsillitis). I also missed a shift once when I had flu and couldn't get out of bed, although I did try; it was so bad I lost over 14lbs in less than a week, and couldn't fall asleep, so within a few days I had started hallucinating. Luckily, the flu started during my annual leave, so I only missed one day of work. Another time, I went into work even though I had the flu. I called a friend and had him help me in to work, because my view was that I could sit down and could use my hands, so I had no excuse not to work. I couldn't visit people, because I could barely stand, but my view was: unless illness stops you being able to do anything, then there is probably some element of your work which you can do, so you should be in work.

At Butlin's I would judge everyone by my standards, whereas in later senior roles, I accepted that everyone has a different standard. From learning about illness and work, and about how the stress of working when ill could prolong the illness, or make other people ill, I accepted that people go off work sick, even where I may choose not to for the same thing. Despite this knowledge, I still wouldn't go off sick unless I physically had been unable to make it into work - even though I knew sometimes that it would probably be best for my health if I did take some time off. To me though, I ended up thinking I was doing the wrong thing if I took sick leave because I was still capable of doing some tasks within work.

In my early job roles, like working at Butlin's, I didn't tell people much about me. I didn't explain about myself to staff; whereas in my later senior roles, I explained to staff, as well as to my own management, what I was like, and that they should pull me up on things if I did something which annoyed them, or if they felt I wasn't behaving as they would like me to behave. One area in which I was aware I lacking, but seemed to struggle to put it right, was giving praise to staff. For some reason, people like to be told they have done well.

I am aware of this when working in therapy sessions or family work, where part of my role in that session involves giving specific praise and acknowledgement when I hear someone describe something that they have done well. I also advise parents to give praise to children to help them to want to do more of what gets good feedback. I also did this in staff supervisions, but I struggled to do it during everyday conversations in the workplace. I would think about how I needed to do this, but for some reason (just like trying to say "I'm fine, how are you?"), I couldn't seem to get the supportive words out. I would get to the end of a work day and suddenly think back and wonder whether I should have given praise or positive feedback or encouragement about things.

I was also not necessarily the best person for offering emotional support. I didn't know really how to do that, but I could listen well and wouldn't get emotionally affected or judgemental about situations. I was good at helping people find solutions to problems, and helping them to look at things from different perspectives.

Over the years, it was fairly common for professionals and parents I would encounter to comment that children with Asperger's would need a lot of support and would be unable to do certain types of work. I used to often explain how I felt those with Asperger's would make great therapists - counter-intuitive, to most people I was talking with. They would think about how those with Asperger's struggled with social situations and with understanding emotional issues, and how they'd often take things very literally. To them, this would mean they would never do any good in jobs with people, especially not jobs where empathy is a key part of the role. I think these traits make someone with Asperger's ideal therapists.

Generally, you don't work with large groups and you aren't socialising; you are in a fake situation where everyone in that situation is playing a role. Most therapists get affected by emotions and the stories clients tell, yet an Asperger's person may well find they remain objective.

I felt these skills made me good at some aspects of management, but not so good at other areas. This also applied to general working. I was always very good when I was given a task and then had to get on with it. I never thought to feed back to my manager though, if I had completed something; I got on with it, did it, and then moved on to the next thing. I couldn't understand why I would need to tell my manager. I had done as I was asked, by the time I was asked to do it.

In fact, communication like that - like keeping a manager informed about what I was doing and progress made or problems encountered - was something I was always terrible at. It wouldn't cross my mind. If I didn't need something from the manager, I wouldn't think to contact them; if I had nothing new to update them on, I wouldn't update them. Managers would tell me I needed to keep them updated, but I would struggle to get the balance right. I would try to do the correct thing of updating them, but then get told I didn't need to update them about every little thing. Without having clear guidance about exactly what was something to share and what wasn't, I had no idea, and often ended up in an all-or-nothing situation where my black and white thinking urged me to tell them everything, or that nothing was important, and that I shouldn't tell them anything.

Before having a diagnosis, I think people just thought I was being awkward, rather than this being a trait of who I am. I would try offering solutions, like having a manager contacting me regularly when they wanted an update; then, they could ask me questions and I would answer what I was asked. This way, hopefully, I would share all that they wanted me to share.

My literalness also impacted on my work. In nearly all my jobs, I have had yearly performance development reviews - and often six-monthly reviews, too - to see how I was progressing towards the targets set. I would read and answer the questions honestly, minimally and literally. I wasn't being awkward; I didn't rush my reviews. I put as much effort in as I could, yet sometimes I would be told that I obviously wasn't taking the process seriously, that my review was so poorly written that I must have just rushed it without any care. I would be told that my answers weren't the correct answers to the questions, and that I needed to sort my attitude out. From my perspective I had given the best and most honest answers I was able to give.

I work well to targets and like statistics and data-gathering, so the performance development review itself worked well for me. I would have targets at the end of my review, which would include things like having to do certain projects or pieces of work. Because of the way I think about things, I would do these as quickly as I could. I have always been someone who completes things straightaway. I don't leave things until the last minute. So, when I did a management training qualification, I completed all coursework at the earliest opportunity - normally the day the work was set, even when I had perhaps three months or more to complete it. I like collecting data on my effectiveness as a practitioner, and looking at areas I could improve to be more effective. The questions I struggled with were things like "Where do you see yourself in five years?" and "What do you want to achieve over the next year?" These were difficult to answer, because I normally didn't know what I wanted to be doing in five years' time; the whole time I was working for employers, I felt that I was drifting along from role to role, knowing I wasn't really doing something I wanted to be doing.

Every job always had too much anxiety; there was always too much interaction with people, and it was not really what I saw in my mind as how I wanted to wake up and spend each day. What I wanted to achieve over the next year was whatever I was told to achieve. I was just working, so I had nothing I wanted to personally achieve - I couldn't understand what they meant by that. I could understand that perhaps some people have performance development reviews and they may want to work up to becoming a manager. They may particularly look at where they are at and what they have to do to become a manager, and then may say they want to achieve some of the things they need to have done to be closer to becoming a manager - like taking on some extra responsibility or attending certain training. Until I found an alternative, though, I just wanted to wake up every day, go into work, get the day over and done with and go home.

I love learning, so any opportunity to attend a course to learn something new, I wanted to take, but I didn't want to do this *in order to* progress, and I couldn't say I wanted do training, because I didn't know what training was going to be available - to be honest, I was happy to attend almost any training. I wanted to just get on with my job and spend most of my time thinking about and doing hypnosis. Inevitably, I would be encouraged to put what the manager wanted me to put on my performance development review, and this would be what I would then aim to achieve across the year in work.

As time went on, I began to feel that working with people therapeutically - care work, or parenting and family support work, or therapy - wasn't really what I wanted to do. I never felt it was what I wanted to do long-term, but I felt I had learnt a lot from working with people about human behaviour; I liked solving problems and I wanted the best for people, but I was encountering a lot of people who were working with me because they were told they had to, and not because they wanted to change their life or circumstances. Doing private therapy, I could just tell the person that I wouldn't work with them if they weren't going to engage in the therapy and if they didn't want to look at making changes, or if they expected me as the therapist to be the one that somehow fixes them, rather than them having to work

191

hard at making and sustaining changes with me supporting them.

But in work, my role was often to work with the family and continue working with them - assertively, if needed - to try to make them make the changes. After more than a decade of this, I was starting to think I didn't want to keep trying to work with people who didn't want my support. I have already mentioned that if someone makes a choice, and that choice has negative consequences, that was their choice and the path they decided to follow. This has always been my attitude and so - although I will always do whatever I can to help the person to be in a position to make better decisions, and help them to have the skills necessary to make more positive choices, and will support them as they make these changes - if they decide that they want to take a different route, then I want to say: "Okay, if you are sure you want to make that decision instead, that is your right and your choice, these are what the consequences could be; I will leave you to it." Then, I'd want to walk away and not invest any more of my time on helping them.

Events in work also began to emphasise that I was different to everyone else. We had course after course, and meeting after meeting, where those presenting would say that if you don't care about the families you are in the wrong job. I never once thought I was working with families because I cared about them. I always want the best for everyone, and will always do what I can to help people have the best outcomes - but I never felt an emotional attachment to any of the families. I liked all the families I worked with in the same way that I have liked all the colleagues I've worked with. People are people; there is no reason not to like anyone, and no reason not to want the best for everyone and to help everyone achieve the best outcomes they can achieve. But at the end of the day, work is just work. You do the work, then after it's done, you do what you want to be doing with your non-work time.

Until it kept being raised as an issue on courses and in meetings, I had never thought that thinking about helping others as just putting my skills of noticing patterns and solving problems to good use to others as a problem. When I voiced that I didn't think about my work as others did, I felt that the responses I got were that I was wrong somehow. I started to feel very different and isolated from everyone else. That is the best way I could describe it. I hardly mixed with anyone, so I didn't feel isolated in that sense, but I was isolated in that I thought differently to everyone else, and felt if I spoke openly about things, I would be criticised for my views rather than being respected and listened to.

This feeling got worse when I had to be part of group clinical supervision. I initially spoke up in supervision, because my views were not the description we were being given about how things 'always' are, or should be. By the end of the first session, the supervisor was singling me out because I thought differently; by the second session, the supervisor was saying they would ask what others think and then come to me because I wasn't likely to agree.

By the third session, I decided I would sit and listen and not join in so much, so I only said a little bit through the supervision. Then, at the end of the supervision, the supervisor said to everyone: "Someone has chosen not to say much this week, how do you all feel about that?" I then went on to say why I hadn't said much, and as I went to speak, the supervisor said: "No, I've asked everyone else to speak, not you." I then listened to other people's views and opinions about why they thought I hadn't said much and how it made them feel. From my perspective, although I felt this was wrong on the supervisor's part, I also felt it would be interesting because I was about to hear what interpretations people had of my silence.

Those who knew me in the room responded with things like, "I know Dan, he is often quiet and doesn't say much, but when he has something to say he will say it. I just assumed this week he didn't have much to say." Those who didn't know me so well said things like, "I hadn't noticed, but now you mention it I am thinking that I hope Dan is okay. Maybe he has other things occupying his mind." There were only about six of us in the session, and many of the members of staff went through line management to say this made them feel uncomfortable. Some staff also spoke to me to say they were feeling uncomfortable with the way the sessions were going. I also fed back to senior management my views and - when we had to feed back whether the first run of supervisions had been helpful, because they were considering bringing the person back to do some more - I said I felt the person shouldn't be brought back, and if they were, I wouldn't want to take part in the supervisions.

The person was brought back to continue doing group clinical supervision, and I didn't take part. This experience contributed heavily to my decision to have an ASD assessment. I felt that if I was able to say I wasn't being awkward, but that I have Asperger's and this is how I think, then maybe I wouldn't have been targeted. I still probably would have been singled out, but perhaps from a more curious angle of seeing what I thought simply because my thinking is different. Maybe people would then be interested to hear my perspective about how I find a way to fit into the wider picture within my own frame or model of the world.

Doing this type of work, I had had senior staff ask me if I had mental problems because of my attitude and responses to things. I had to reply that I had nothing diagnosed. I would be honest with people about what I could and couldn't do, and what helped me to work best. Some of what I struggle with may seem trivial to others, yet they are huge struggles to me, and I would be treated as if I was just trying to be awkward. For example, to me, making a telephone call is a huge thing. It can take me days, sometimes weeks, to make a phone call, and sometimes I never end up managing to do it. Answering the phone is also a challenge, even if it is my wife calling me, to whom I am more than happy to talk.

Some things make it easier for me to make phone calls, like having a quiet, private place to make the call where no-one is listening in and I can't see anyone else around me - and it's the same with receiving calls. The more isolated I am, the more comfortable I am to receive the call and talk on the phone. I can sometimes make and receive calls straightaway, but I feel extreme anxiety doing this. I have to try to focus everything out of my awareness apart from the phone call, and have to try to hold this focus. I become very monosyllabic and I struggle to process what I am hearing on the phone call. This only gets worse if I start noticing distractions, noises or speech of others around me, and because I am trying so hard to hold it together, I can become very blunt and abrupt with people around me if they don't keep away.

All of these different work experiences were what led me to seeking an ASD diagnosis. I'd reached a point where I felt the only way I was going to be treated as an individual was if I had a label I could tell people that made them listen and look at what could help me work best - rather than to simply dismiss my views and feelings. I had always hoped that people would treat everyone as individuals, and would as far as possible look at how they can be helped in areas they struggle with - whether it means that adaptations need to be made to the work environment, or that additional support is needed in certain areas, or that they have more focus on the tasks they can do, while taking on more of the tasks that play to their strengths. I was always good with statistics, and liked analysing data - and I liked having projects to work on, like creating courses. But other staff didn't like these areas. They may, on the other hand, have been very good at making phone calls, and arranging meetings.

When I met my first wife, she wasn't keen on me doing hypnosis. She found it scary, so I didn't do much. I still read some books, but I did my best to keep my focus off hypnosis. My main interest during that time was focusing on psychology, and learning about people and different mental health problems, and I continued with my interest in learning about the different sciences. When my first wife and I separated, I almost immediately picked up where I left off with my interest in hypnosis. As a teenager, I had done hypnosis and read books on it, but I hadn't taken any courses or anything, because they were too expensive. Now, I took my first actual hypnosis qualification.

The first qualification I passed was a home study diploma in Curative Hypnotherapy, followed by a live hypnotherapy diploma. I have continued to study hypnotherapy ever since 2001, when I took that first home study. In 2001, I started working with clients doing one-to-one hypnotherapy sessions. By 2004 I had taken dozens of hypnotherapy and neuro-linguistic programming (NLP) training courses, and various other wellbeing courses. I was recording sessions with people, which I would watch back and analyse to see what was going on - what I was doing, what the interaction with the client was like, what I'd missed and could have done, and what I might do in the future. I had therapeutic sessions video recorded, with the permission of the client, and practice sessions recorded, where I would mainly be practicing hypnotic techniques with people.

Recording to learn wasn't a new thing to me. While I was with my first wife, I used to have my best friend over to visit regularly, and another person we know. My wife would go to bed and I would set up a video camera and record our evenings of just talking and drinking; while talking and drinking, I would be practicing influencing the other two. I would then watch the video footage back to see what worked best and where I could improve my influencing skills. I had learnt that to be an effective hypnotist, you needed to be able to understand non-verbal behaviour - this was just my way of practicing and learning about non-verbal behaviour, by practicing covert influence. I also recorded a lot of self-hypnosis tracks which I would listen to, so that I could get a sense of what it was like to be hypnotised by me - what worked and what didn't work.

It could seem unusual, having someone with poor social skills who struggles to understand emotions and takes things literally working as a hypnotherapist. But a therapy session isn't a social setting; there are rules and structures to how things are done. I feel nervous entering into social situations, and want to find a corner and sit quietly, hoping that no-one notices me. I have no problem doing a therapy session with a client, even in front of an audience of students, yet I know people who have trained as therapists but still don't have the confidence to work with clients. Taking things literally can be helpful in therapy, because what most people don't realise is how much we give away non-verbally. Thinking about it literally, this can be helpful to gaining deeper understanding of people.

For example: a client may be talking about how they need help because they suffer with stress and find they have anxiety attacks. As you ask them about different parts of their life, you notice that when you mention their relationship with their partner, they rub their neck and tell you everything is fine there, the partner is very supportive. Then a bit later you ask about the partner again and see the client rub their neck again.

This may seem insignificant, but as a therapist I made an observation when I first asked about the partner of the client who rubbed their neck. Taking this literally as 'the person may have a pain in the neck' - and being aware that this is a common saying that people will use to describe others who annoy them - I linked the pain they experience in the neck at the time of thinking about the partner as possibly connected. To test this, I talked about other unrelated things and then came back to talking about the partner again, just to if the client did the same action again.

If they did the action regardless of what I talked, it was probable that they genuinely did have a pain in the neck - rubbing the neck happened to coincide with talking about a partner, and so was unlinked. But if the neck rubbing only happened when talking about the partner, I would be more confident that something about the partner annoyed them. It could have been that they didn't consciously know what annoyed them about the partner - and I wouldn't want to put ideas in their mind if my interpretation was wrong - so I would just be mindful of this information as an extra aspect to help me understand the situation better.

Had I pushed this line directly, they may have had good reasons why they didn't want to tell me, or they may not have known at all - how could someone not know their own partner is a pain in the neck? - but we view the world through the trance we are living in, so someone in love can become consciously blind to behaviours that their loved one does which don't fit within their view of the world. Milton Erickson once said that the quickest way to make someone fall out of love is to have them start focusing on every small detail and flaw. Until someone does this, they may be unaware of all the flaws in their partner.

One thing you have to watch out for as someone with Asperger's doing therapy, is that the therapy session is supposed to be all about the client; the client should be the centre of your world while you are working with them. So, for me, I like hypnosis, and I could talk about hypnosis endlessly, but in a therapy session it isn't about me and my interests. The client isn't seeing me to learn about hypnosis. I have to focus on the fact that I am 'doing' hypnosis, rather than 'talking' about it, necessarily. If a client asks about hypnosis I have to work hard to be as precise as I can at answering their questions without taking it as an excuse to be allowed to talk for the rest of the session about hypnosis. I have to bring the focus back to the client and what is relevant to helping them.

That doesn't mean that there are never times when talking about hypnosis is the relevant thing, but the focus should always be on the client and on how every moment in the session should be used to be helpful to the client, not to meet my needs and talk about what I am interested in.

Working as a therapist is a great way to learn new skills and continue to develop my abilities at understanding people, recognising different behavioural responses, and practicing communication skills. I also get to look for patterns and solve problems, and generally it is a very solitary experience. When I used to do hypnotherapy out of a therapy centre, I used to love the time between clients when I was sitting alone in the centre; if the day was nice enough I would sit at the back door, resting, looking over the small garden area, and feeling the warmth of the sun on my face. Then time would fly by during the 90-minute therapy session with a client, before I could sit alone, relaxing some more.

Although I like doing hypnosis - and like solving problems and looking for patterns - I don't particularly like doing therapy, because my focus during therapy isn't on me and my interests, it is on the client and how I can help them. This is alright for a while, but spending all my time doing this is like spending all my time having to keep a part of me quiet, which takes a lot of mental effort; then, I almost feel I over-compensate as soon as the opportunity arises by focusing endlessly on hypnosis outside of therapy sessions... This means my wife has to hear me constantly talking about hypnosis, and having me watching hypnosis videos, and listening to hypnosis audio recordings, and reading hypnosis books, and doing hypnosis at every opportunity I get.

For years, I would practice hypnosis techniques and skills everywhere. I still do from time to time, but now I spend more time in my own mind thinking about hypnosis scenarios. When travelling on buses, I used to practice my observation skills by watching how people were breathing, and then would practice hypnotising them by matching their breathing and then beginning to guide the other person into hypnosis. I also used to do this in cafes and when I was out and about, sitting on benches. I would also practice noticing when people were naturally entering hypnosis, and then gently deepening these natural everyday trance states.

In many of the jobs I have had, I have taught courses - from behaviour management, conflict resolution and restraint training, to relaxation skills and stress management. In my family and parenting support roles, I have taught courses including parenting skills, solution-focused working, and working with resistant families. I have also run courses and groups for parents and teenagers on topics like parenting and child/teen, to parent domestic abuse. After a few years of doing hypnotherapy I started teaching courses, too: some training courses on topics like the healing power of storytelling, and hypnosis courses, and therapeutic groups on topics like self-hypnosis and overcoming phobias or post-traumatic stress disorder. I began to realise that I preferred holding courses to doing therapy. Courses allowed me to share my knowledge and talk about what I know, with people who also wanted to know what I know.

I don't like being around lots of people, or being around people often, so I wouldn't want to run courses all the time, and I still prefer courses with small groups of people. I like giving talks as well, because it allows me to talk about what I am interested in, and to answer questions about what I like talking about. One challenge I have always found with running courses is that I don't remember people's names. I have run courses where I see the same people for multiple days in a row - or even week after week - and still I have no idea who they are. Unless there is something I find interesting about someone, I don't care what their name is, so I don't remember it.

Many people have asked me whether I find talks and courses difficult to present because of my having Asperger's and struggling in social situations. I explain that I don't, because they aren't social situations. If I am teaching a group of people, I'm giving information. If it is a course, I am likely to set tasks for people to do - or I may do demonstrations, but even then, I am still talking to people and telling them what to do. Any questions that come from an audience are either things I know the answer to or I don't know the answer and so I'm likely to learn something new. If I am holding a talk, I am just talking to a group, and again potentially responding to questions. If I am less sure about a subject, or if I have to be too structured, under certain circumstances I can be anxious, but I think this is normal when people are presenting.

Presenting involves doing certain behaviours to make the audience feel you are talking to them, but it isn't the same as socialising, and it definitely isn't the same as being at a social event. If I am talking to a group, usually the group is quiet and listening. If I am talking to someone at a social event, there are probably many people talking around us.

I like learning and sharing knowledge; teaching allows me to do this. I have often said to people that I would love to be a documentary presenter for the same reason: I could go and interview people about the topic they are specialist in, researching and investigating subjects, and then sharing my findings with people. I have tried to interview people I respect within the hypnosis community, and have interviewed authors about their books as a way of learning and gaining insight, and sharing knowledge with others. This is also why I started sharing knowledge online.

Back in the late 1990s, I downloaded Elvis Presley's 'laughing version' of *Are You Lonesome Tonight?* as an mp3. I was so impressed that you could download music that I told a friend it would be the future; I told him I wanted to set up an online record business. I said there were dozens of great bands in Bognor Regis alone who wrote and performed their own songs. I explained that, if there was an online record company, to which bands could sign up to a royalty share, and thereby they could have the songs available to be downloaded by the public, they could reach a far wider audience.

Unfortunately, I didn't have the skills to do this and no-one seemed to think it was a good idea at the time. The comment I always got back was that an MP3 player can only fit the equivalent of a CD album, and even then, they cost hundreds of pounds; downloadable music wouldn't be 'a thing' when people can buy music on cassette tapes and CDs for cheap. By 2001, I was making meditation MP3s, but I didn't know how they could be made downloadable. I was also telling everyone that e-paper would lead to people having portable devices with e-paper screens to read books on. Again, no-one believed me. By 2004, I was selling MP3 downloads and short downloadable ebooks as ways of sharing knowledge and helping people.

I felt streaming web videos (what people would now call webinars) were likely to be a thing since 3G internet came in, so in about 2006, myself and a friend started holding live hypnosis webinars, and I started a YouTube channel sharing hypnosis information and self-hypnosis videos. I built a website where MP3 versions of the self-hypnosis videos could be downloaded, and I also had meditations designed to be downloaded by commuters onto 3G mobile phones. The idea was that someone commuting who was stressed from the day could buy a ten-minute guided meditation to listen to on the journey home, to help them relax and separate the work part from the home part of their day.

As technology got faster and worked better, I started exploring teaching via technology. Initially, I had downloadable audio courses and ebooks for sale, and a couple of downloadable training videos too. Then, I found a website which allowed me to make print books and put them up for sale on Amazon, and also available in most other bookshops, so I started writing books to be sold in print. This wasn't vanity publishing, but a new up-and-coming way of publishing, called print on demand, where a customer orders a book and the publishing company prints that one copy of the book and sends it to the customer. There is no stock held by the author or anyone else; there is thus no need to buy many copies of your own book, and no need to personally fulfil orders. This changed my focus from making a living by having to work face-to-face with people, which is an uncomfortable thing, to making income online - both from teaching online courses and as an author. My main focus was writing books as a way of sharing knowledge, both in print and as ebooks, and more recently, I found a company which has allowed me to make online training courses.

Making income as an author is ideal for me as someone with Asperger's. Writing can be a very solitary process. I get to spend plenty of time alone. I can do research and learn new things, I can write and share my knowledge, and I don't often have to come into contact with people. Making online courses is my second focus; it isn't quite as good, because I have to interact with people more, and I have to make sure that students are getting what they want out of their training, but I can still largely be solitary doing that.

Over the 21 years that I have been a working adult, it is only now that I feel I am settling into a work role with which I am comfortable. I think a lot of people with Asperger's end up gravitating to writing as a preferred way of making a living, because when you do have to interact with people, it is normally via email or messaging. I think the other career which people with Asperger's like to end up working in is with nature in some way: either with animals or perhaps in a gardening- or forestry-type role. I know I would love to spend every day alone in the woods if I could, and would do a nature job if the right type of role ever presented itself.

# CHAPTER SIX

## *Who Am I Now?*

Currently I'm in my late 30's. I feel that I have become very mindful of who I am and of what my flaws are. I have learnt a lot over the years about communication, but I still have certain aspects of myself I think I would like to change. One of the challenges is that what is a problem in one setting is a strength in another, and if I changed aspects of myself, I could end up not being me.

I have faced discrimination, and have been powerless to do anything about it - which is what led me to seek an ASD diagnosis. I have also upset people because of the way I can communicate, and have struggled to overcome my black and white thinking, and to understand and follow what others would deem to be the correct behaviours for certain situations.

I like spending time alone. Most people tell me they struggle to be alone for too long. In many of the flats in which I have lived I have had a small windowless toilet/shower room. Not only am I comfortable being alone, and seek out solitude, but I also like being alone in an enclosed dark place. When I first lived alone in my own studio flat I had no electricity during the winter. This meant that once the sun set, the flat was dark. Despite this, I still used to sit in the toilet/shower room on the toilet with no light on. It is difficult to explain but there is something about the sound and the feel of being in the room that was relaxing. The flat I lived in was quiet. I rarely heard sounds of neighbours, and with windows closed, I couldn't hear anything outside the flat - yet the sound was still different in the shower room. I would sit in there for hours on end; it wouldn't take long to lose track of time. Even when it was winter, in the evening, I would choose to sit in the shower room, rather than on a sofa or lying in bed.

Still today, I will sit in my bathroom in the dark for hours at a time. I can be in there for four or five hours and feel like just twenty minutes have passed. Sometimes, when I have had a stressful time and I am feeling like I need to escape everything for a while, my wife has made me a den in the lounge by draping blankets over the backs of chairs, and I will curl up in the den and relax. The den isn't dark like the bathroom, but the light is diffused from all directions through the blankets which reduces stimuli. For a quick and easy solution, I will often build a 'sofa tent': I will throw a blanket over the back of the sofa and drape it hanging down over the front of the sofa, creating a small 'one-man' tent which I will then climb into, cover myself over, and relax in. I used to do this when I worked for one of the children's home companies. When working for that company, staff used to have to sleep in the lounge and dining room. Every night, after the children went to bed, we would drag out mattresses, and set up our beds, with one sleeping in the dining room and the other in the lounge. I used to ask if I could sleep in the lounge so that I could set up my 'sofa tent' which I would then lay in.

For as long as I can remember, I have had what some might see as a sleep problem. So, when I lay in the 'sofa tent', I wouldn't be going to sleep - rather, it was just somewhere comfortable to be. Often, I would listen to self-hypnosis or meditation tracks for most of the night. I remember when I was in secondary school and we had to do a 'day in the life of...' project in English where we had to write what our day consisted of. I wrote how I woke up about 6am and started the day by watching cartoons. As soon as a programme is made into a cartoon, it seems to instantly make the programme better. I used to find most live action programmes boring and difficult to follow and understand, yet cartoons would entertain me. I would then go to school, and after school I would go home, change, and then go out. If I had something I was doing - like martial arts or playing pool, or swimming, or youth club - then I would do this, if not, when I lived in Warningcamp I would go into the woods; when I lived in Littlehampton I would go to the beach. In the evening when I returned home I would sit in my bedroom reading non-fiction books and often watching Open University programmes late into the night, normally not going to sleep before 2 or 3am.

I always felt I worked better later in the evening. The only exception to easily getting up early came when I was in my late teens while working at Butlin's when I suddenly (and it was very confusing for me) started having difficulties getting up on time in the morning. I would wake up about 8am if I didn't have an alarm set, and even with the alarm set it was common for me to turn the alarm off, go back to sleep and wake up at about 8am with no memory of turning the alarm off. During this phase in my life, I had to set the alarm across the other side of my bedroom so that I would have to physically walk to turn it off. During my twenties, I rarely felt tired. It was common for me to stay awake for days at a time, sometimes I would stay awake for six days and then on the seventh day, I would get about eight hours' sleep, wake without an alarm clock and feel rested and refreshed enough to do the same again. During my early twenties, I lived by the seafront, so at times I would wait until my first wife was asleep and - because I was still wide awake - I would walk over to the beach and sit and gaze out to sea for hours before heading back in as morning approached.

When my best friend stayed over, we would both go out to the beach. One night, we stood on the water's edge. It was a calm night; we watched the sun set, and a blanket of stars appear overhead. We listened to the gentle lashing of the water on the sand. We spoke about philosophy, the universe, and consciousness all night long, walking forward with the water as the tide went out, and walking back with the water as the tide came in again during the morning, and watched the sun rise. We then went inside, sorted ourselves out for the day and got on. My best friend struggled through the day, because he was tired, whereas I had no problem going through the day, and fully expected to do the same the next night.

Nowadays, I need more sleep than I did in my teens (apart from that one brief period - teenagers usually go through a stage where their body clocks shift and they wake later and go to bed later, but unfortunately the school system still expects them to be in early and in a functional state, which is going against a teen's biology) or in my twenties. I had no problem getting three or four hours' sleep per night on average during those years. I worked in residential children's homes during my twenties. I would be on shift at 8am and it was common for it to take until perhaps 2am to get the teenagers to bed - and then we had to do the paperwork, which could take a couple of hours. Still, we would have to be up about 7am to start waking the teens up, and to put out breakfast and prepare for the handover to staff coming on shift. It was a good night if we managed to get the teenagers to bed by midnight, and normally the first thing you think of once they are in bed is that it must be time for a cup of tea, and then we'll do the paperwork. So, even on a good night, we usually didn't get to bed until 2am.

Most nights, I set an alarm. as my wife has to wake up at a certain time for work. Without an alarm I usually will wake up anywhere between 7am and 8am. I usually feel at my best late in the evening. Sometimes I can start to feel tired about 9pm, but this quickly passes. When I have tried to go to bed at this time when I am feeling tired, I find that I can't actually sleep. I usually go to bed about midnight, but over half the time I will take many hours to fall asleep. I don't really worry, so I'm not lying in bed having anxious thoughts, but I do often have ideas. I will lie in bed and suddenly think of an idea, and will then start examining this idea and seeing how it would play out. It could be an idea about a science problem, or a new idea for a book or a course. Unlike a worry, which can usually be written down as a sentence - and perhaps the solution can be written down, or it can be identified that there isn't a solution within the individual's control - an idea would just turn into a night-time of exploring and expanding upon that idea. If I was alone, then this would be fine, but I live with my wife, and it is preferable if we live in the same time zones.

As mentioned, when I was single, I would be up for days at a time; if I was single now, I would probably get up at these times when I have these thoughts, and because they totally wake me up, I would work on the idea; only once I was tired would I then go to bed. I would probably live in a dark place with no reference to time, so that I would sleep when I was tired and work when I was awake. I have always been curious as to what pattern I would fall into if I was in a timeless space like this, and what my perception would be of time. Part of the beauty of the internet is that it is timeless. By that, I mean there are people from all over the world online, so if I wanted to interact with people about my ideas and about hypnosis, I could probably be online at any time of the day and find someone to interact with. Generally, I am happy not interacting with people, but some of my best ideas are developed and fleshed out by having someone there as a sounding board - often someone who doesn't fully understand what I'm talking about, so they ask me questions which help me to cement it in my mind better and see it more clearly. It is helpful when the person who is a sounding board wants to know what the applications or possibilities are for the idea, which allows me to explore these more fully than I can from within my rigid box of a brain.

I have always liked patterns. I like things to be just right. There was a time when someone asked me if I had obsessive compulsive disorder (OCD) because I wanted everything just right. I explained that I knew I didn't have OCD, because I had no anxiety associated with wanting things just right. I didn't think anything bad would happen if things weren't just right; I just felt a compulsion to want things correct. People have asked me whether I live in a spotless home because of wanting things just right, and I tell them I don't. I like to live in a tidy home, but it isn't spotless. I have little motivation for tidying, dusting and vacuuming. This was the same when I was younger - I liked everything just right but that didn't mean spotless: I can have all my books exactly where and how I want them; I can have my DVD and Blu-ray collection in the correct order; I can have my magazines in the right places. But I don't care if there is some dust on a windowsill, or if the floor needs vacuuming. If there are clearly defined bits of dirt on the floor, I will bend down and pick them up, and if there are too many then I will vacuum, but it is about the patterns in things that is important.

My wife refers to my side of the bed as my floordrobe. I have clothes on my side of the bed exactly as I want them to be, but to my wife, I have clothes on the floor that should either be in the wash basket, or put away in a drawer or wardrobe. I am often told that the floor isn't a wardrobe, but then she has me moaning at her if I go into the bedroom and can't see my clothes that I left on the floor, because it means I struggle to find them, and when I need them, I will usually ask her if she knows where they are and if she can get them for me. The same goes with magazines. I will have new science magazines - I have a pile of unread magazines, usually on the kitchen surface where I can find them, and in my office, I will have a pile of my most recently read magazines. My wife's opinion is that the kitchen work surface isn't a magazine holder, and so from time to time she will tidy up and move my magazines in to my office, normally just clumping things together. I then have to hunt for those magazines and separate them out, and normally I leave them on top of my laptop until I have read them, but in the meantime any new magazines I buy end up back in the kitchen.

Even in shops, cafes and restaurants, I like everything to be where it should and how it should be. I used to catch the bus from outside a furniture store. Every day, I would stand at the bus stop and struggle to look in the window of the store, because they had a sunset painting upside down. Every day I thought to myself that I was sure they would correct this. I was catching the bus early in the morning, so the shop was never open when I was at the bus stop. Eventually I went past the shop while it was open, and couldn't help myself. I had to get them to sort out the picture, so I went in and found the first member of staff I could. They were serving customers at the time, so I interrupted and told them I was in a hurry but I just wanted to let them know that the sunset picture in the window was upside down. I said to them that it had been for weeks and they needed to have it hung up the correct way. The next time I passed the shop the picture was up the correct way.

When I go into restaurants and cafes, I find myself pushing in the chairs correctly under the tables. I used to stack crockery correctly on the tables as well, but fortunately I have generally stopped doing this; it used to be time-consuming getting in or out of places. Even with pushing chairs correctly under the tables, I now usually only do this to chairs I am walking past. I try not to notice anything further than arm's reach. At home, I don't like all the washing up just 'thrown' into the sink. It should be stacked correctly beside the sink, ready to be washed up, not in the sink, and things should be placed in cupboards and boxes in specific ways that make logical sense and best utilise the space.

I have had problems when packing to move home; I would pack boxes like I'm playing Tetris, and would have each box packed solidly. Boxes of books or magazines become almost immovable due to the sheer weight of them. I will think that using as few boxes as possible so that there are less boxes to carry is the best way to go, but then you have perhaps a dozen large book-filled boxes, rather than sixty small manageable boxes.

My wife would describe me as having an obsession with learning and knowledge. I will try to watch almost every documentary I can - the reason why we don't have Sky TV. If we did, I would probably never get anything done. I also like to keep a copy of every documentary I watch, so that I can watch it again. Some things I can watch repeatedly. I try not to do this nowadays, because it would take up all of my time. Years ago, I would watch the same film or documentary multiple times every day. If someone asked me about it, I would struggle to describe it, unless asked about specific facts, but if I was watching it, I could say what was about to happen or what someone was about to say - even years later.

I don't want to die, not because I am afraid of dying, but because dying means I will miss out on gaining new knowledge. My main interest, and the thing I talk most about, is still hypnosis, but I want to know everything I can about all the sciences. I keep every *BBC Focus* magazine I buy, just like I keep every *New Scientist* magazine, and many other science magazines. I used to have paper copies of every *Scientific American* and *Scientific American Mind* magazine, but I have many of these as PDFs now so I got rid of the paper copies. I don't want to get rid of these magazines because they are full of knowledge - although, as people keep telling me, so is the internet. To me, I don't know what I want to know, I want to be able to look through and discover. Or if I suddenly think of something, I want to know that I know where I saw it. I don't work so well searching the internet for what I want to find; I work better having a mental map of where I saw it and thinking 'I remember seeing something about that in the *BBC Focus* magazine with this front cover' and then searching for it. It is like when I found the first care job I did by looking on the boards at all of the jobs, taking it all in and finding what I was looking for... This is easier for me than looking at a screen of options to narrow down my search, leading to more boxes to narrow my search further, and the whole time I don't really know what I am trying to narrow down to - or what I am missing and eliminating by not choosing other options.

Science is full of patterns, and some of those patterns haven't yet been solved. These interest me. I can spend hours in my own mind thinking about them and filling notebooks with ideas, trying to figure out simple solutions. I believe most problems have simple solutions - even solutions that look complex, when looked at in the right way, can suddenly be seen as quite simple. This goes for much of the complexities of the work of Dr Milton Erickson. His treatments were often radical; there are many books written about his work and trying to analyse his thinking and how he came up with such radical and personalised treatments. One thing is that he had years of knowledge, so his earlier treatment ideas - although radical - weren't necessarily always spontaneous, they were well thought out. But as a pattern, to understand how he came to his conclusions, all you need to think about is three principles: what the goal is, what you are observing, and how you can utilise your observations in the direction of the goal. For therapy, this takes clinical knowledge of problems clients present, but if you are willing to open up to observations from all of your senses and on all levels that the client is communicating, suddenly you have ideas which seem radical, yet were based on three very simple principles that anyone could have applied. Any therapist could record a client session which includes lots of information-gathering and conversation, and watch that session repeatedly. They could observe the language the client uses, tonal changes as they speak and say certain words, metaphors and stories they use when describing the problem and solution, body language, head movements and gestures used while talking and listening, and plenty of other such information. They could use this to formulate ideas for treatment, which could be a task based on a metaphor or idea the client used; it could be a certain reframe given, or any number of different types of therapeutic input.

Some of my behavioural traits can be awkward at times. I find myself mimicking certain sounds. I don't know why, and I don't know what it is about those sounds. It could be an accent that someone has, through to the sound of a bird singing in the trees. I think it is that I find something about the sound comforting - and the repetition of the sound comforting. I don't know for sure that this is the reason I mimic sounds, because some sounds have a certain pattern to them that feels good to mimic, but the sound itself can be annoying. The SMS sound for example is one I can't help but mimic, or the sound of certain mobile phone ring tones, or certain phrases people use. The phrase may annoy me, but the sound of it resonates, and I find myself copying it over and over again. I have to try really hard to keep mimicking in my mind when I'm in public. I can easily find myself making the sound of someone's mobile phone, or of a phrase they have used; sometimes, the person will hear me and be offended and think I am making fun of them, when that isn't my intention at all.

It isn't so bad when I'm copying animal sounds, like bird songs; it just sounds like I am whistling. It may irritate people, but I don't think it offends them. I also find myself copying the sounds of objects like cars or coffee machines. I don't think afterwards: do people think I am strange? No-one in that context has ever said I am strange, so I don't know. But I spend time trying to analyse my behaviour, trying to learn who I am, what I do, and how it may be perceived, as well as how I can control these parts of me. One way I have learnt to have some control over this part of me is to go inside my mind at these times, and to copy the sound in my head. This is difficult to do when I need to be focusing on doing something else. So if I have a compulsion to make the sound of the coffee machine when I am in a coffee shop ordering a drink and it is my turn to order, if I am in my mind copying the sound, I struggle to process both that and making the order. I have enough trouble making the order as it is, without the added complication of being inside my mind doing something else when I need to be outside my mind, interacting with someone. The situation will influence which option I choose. I may be in a queue, waiting to be served, when I hear a sound; if in that split second I don't think I'm about to be served, I may go into my mind to make the sound, but then I may have been wrong, and may now get served. Or if I think I'm about to be served I may start making the sound out loud, and then pause mid-flow to make my order, and then continue making the sound. This pause can make me extra impatient. All I want to do is get the order out of the way so that I can complete the sound. I sometimes cross-match the pattern, so I may physically tap out the sound or do a movement for the sound rather than verbally mimic it.

I don't like incomplete patterns. Humans are pattern-matching creatures; this is something we excel at. If I hear part of a pattern, I want to complete it. So if someone taps out 'tap, tap tap-tap, tap', I want to go 'tap, tap'. I can do this in my mind or out loud, I can complete patterns physically, verbally or internally. Sometimes the pattern is a mobile phone ringing and the person quickly answers the phone which interrupts the pattern, so I complete it. Or the pattern could happen accidentally in the environment - the way someone is putting plates down on a table, for example, may inadvertently make the start of a pattern.

Some patterns I can find incredibly annoying. I feel myself getting angrier and angrier, the longer the pattern continues. I don't know why this is, but I feel my reaction is extreme; it is as if someone is assaulting my senses. I will cover my ears, I will close my eyes. All I want to do is escape the sight or sound. Stupidly, in some of the situations there is a simple answer that isn't an answer I take. I just sit there getting angrier. The sound the microwave makes when it is done is one such sound. Old microwaves I used to have would count down and then give one ding. Now the microwave counts down and then repeatedly beeps to let you know it has finished; it does this for what feels like ages, but is probably only a minute or so. The washing machine does the same when it finishes its cycle, as does the tumble dryer - all with different patterns of beeping. The simple answer is to go and turn them off when they make a noise, but this is rarely what I do. I don't know what it is about these sounds that cause me so much distress. As I write this, I wonder whether they all beep with a similar tonal range, or whether there is some other connection between the sounds. At home, there are eight solar-powered objects - like a monkey, an elephant, and a flower - that make a regular ticking noise all day, every day. I don't get fazed by these, whether it is one, two three or any other amount of them ticking. When there is more than one ticking, the ticks aren't synchronised with each other, which I also don't mind.

When I was younger I used to have a clock that ticked continuously and also played a tune every fifteen minutes. It would play the first part of the tune at quarter past the hour, 50% of the tune at half past the hour, 75% of the tune at quarter to the hour, and 100% of the tune on the hour, followed by chiming the number of hours. It did this from 6am until midnight every day. My wife hated it, but I found it relaxing and comforting. It is confusing why some sounds cause such a strong negative reaction, while others cause comfort or no significant reaction, despite them seeming so similar. One thing I liked about the clock, and about analogue watches, was the second hand, the pendulum and other moving parts. I would enjoy watching the regularity of the movement. The regular movement would draw me in and relax me, like rocking in a chair or swinging gently in a swing, or a tree swaying in the wind as a child. I find watching regular movements - especially slow ones - relaxing. I also find the same when I make slow movements, or movements which seem to fall into a pattern that takes on a life of its own. I often find myself beating out rhythms with my hands, or tapping rhythms with my feet that take on a life of their own. I also make regular slow movements. Some movements are things like intentionally enjoying the feeling of consciously breathing in a slow and rhythmical way, others can be moving my head or eyes, and some are more obvious like tapping my foot or shaking my leg, or drumming or clicking my fingers.

There is something magical about movement, especially slow meaningful movement. When I was young, I started forming an interest in Tai Chi because it looked to me like the martial arts I saw in films - but slowed down and done with each element of the move being intentionally carried out. Martial arts plays a big part in my internal world. My two favourite martial arts are Wing Chun and Aikido, with Wing Chun being about directness and Aikido being about circles and indirectness. With Wing Chun, someone may attack, and the Wing Chun practitioner may simultaneously deflect that attack in the process of creating an opening and striking in that opening, taking the shortest route possible. It is economical in its approach. Someone attacking an Aikido practitioner, meanwhile, may find the practitioner gently taking hold of the attacking hand as they turn, directing that hand along a circle until the hand reaches a point on the circle where the attacker is now being thrown due to the twist that has appeared in their wrist. The energy came from the attacker, and went back to the attacker. I have always found that these two approaches sum up hypnosis and therapy, where you absorb and give back some things, but find an opening and deliver a clear direct message about other things.

When I listen to music, I find that it usually stimulates choreographed martial arts mental imagery, or storytelling playing out in my mind. I'm sure this is very common, but my life is played to a backdrop of almost constant music and tunes. I don't necessarily know the tunes; they are just always there as if my life is a musical. This may be why I like musicals - because that is just how I feel life is. When I'm walking along a street, the state of mind I'm in will have music playing to it, which will in turn influence the speed I walk and how I act as I walk. Everything in life has a rhythm; every action has a rhythm. When I used to be in violent situations when working in residential children's homes, I would be handling situations - perhaps blocking punches or kicks, or dealing with someone trying to stab me or cut me with a knife, or attacking me with a baseball bat. I may be having to restrain them using various techniques to ensure their safety and the safety of others around; I was always trying to avoid situations which may result in needing to involve the police, which could lead to the teenager becoming criminalised. The whole time, I would have tunes playing in my mind and be 'dancing' to the rhythms. All my movements would be choreographed to make the tune playing in my mind match what is going on.

It may sound unusual, but this inner experience isn't just a tune. I see an alternate reality. I know it isn't what my eyes see, but it is like having a director's view of my life, as well as an actor's view of my life. I imagine things like camera angle changes, and lighting changes, and music getting louder or softer - or picking up or slowing down tempo. I can imagine the camera panning back and up from a scene, or zooming in, close up. Sometimes my inner world sneaks out and I find myself whistling or humming, or even singing bits of tunes. I don't necessarily know what the tunes are, and they can be something I don't think I have ever heard - it is just what is there in that moment.

Probably one of the most annoying aspects of myself that I would like to change is the way I respond to situations. Generally, I find things difficult which others would say are small and not stressful. I will respond by getting highly stressed, and will often overreact and want to escape the situation. On the other hand, things that others say they wouldn't be able to handle, I have no problem with. If I walk in to a shop, I can quickly find just being in the shop stressful. If the temperature in the shop isn't correct, this is stressful. If the shop is too crowded or cramped, this is stressful. If the lights are too bright, or flicker, this is stressful. If staff members try talking to me or engaging with me when I haven't asked them to, this is stressful. If there is loud music, or loud noises in the shop, or sounds of children, this is stressful.

All of this stress is just the background stress of being in the shop. The stress is amplified with time, and if I have to do anything in the shop. If I am buying something, I have to go to the till to be served; this will increase stress levels. I find it difficult to talk with someone during this time. I need to focus on the task of queuing and monitoring when it is my turn to walk forward to the till, and then I need to focus all of my attention on the purchasing process, and on using the card reader, or paying with cash. Card readers are much more stressful than paying with cash.

Stress increases further still if the person serving doesn't just take the items I am buying, scan them and have them bagged - which now is normally done by the customer as we bring our own bags. If the person serving starts asking whether I want to 'save 20% on my shopping today' and proceeds to try to tell me I should have a store card, or if they start asking me whether I want to buy any of the items they have around the till, my stress levels increase and I become more blunt and abrupt with the person serving to speed them along and make them just do as I want them to do. If I had wanted extra items or a store card, I would have asked.

I struggle to ask for the bill in restaurants. I never know what to say or how to get the attention of the waiting staff. I usually get my wife to ask for the bill, or to go up and order food in pubs, or to pay after we have eaten. When we are out in a pub or a restaurant, I don't like to be pestered by the staff. I like to be served and then left alone; but I do want the staff to be attentive to our needs, and to be able to watch for behavioural cues that let them know whether we want them to come to our table. I don't like being given my food and then five minutes later, just as I have a mouthful of food, they come back and ask if everything is alright. My wife usually responds to this by nodding, smiling and saying, "Yes, it's lovely, thanks." Which I think is just her being polite. I normally just smile or ignore their presence. I would never say the food is lovely because I don't think that about any food I have ever eaten - food is an energy source, it isn't something that is 'lovely'.

On my wife's birthday a couple of years ago, we went to a restaurant with a number of other people. The waitress brought over a gift for my wife and said it was from the restaurant. She liked this; I was already deducting tips in my mind. A bit later in the evening, she came over with something else, so I was deducting more tips and was beginning to get irritated, yet my wife seemed to like this behaviour. This went on repeatedly throughout the evening, with the waitress offering to take photographs of the group, engaging and laughing with us, commenting positively about gifts my wife had received, and bringing free items over for the group. All I wanted was for the waitress to bring over the food as required and keep quiet. My wife loved the service we received; I hated it.

The most stressful food outlet service is in fast food restaurants, where I have been mentally rehearsing saying my order for the whole time I have been queuing. I then get to the counter, I say the order exactly as I have been mentally rehearsing it, with nothing vague about what I have said. "A medium quarter pounder with cheese meal with diet coke, and a medium chicken burger meal with orange juice," I'd say, and the person serving would reply "Was that a large meal?"

I have already said I want a medium meal… Then, they will ask "What drinks do you want with that?" Again, I will already have told them. By this point, I can't remember. My brain doesn't work like that. I was remembering it by repeating it over and over again while I was queuing. Once I'd said what my order was, I forgot what my order was. Verbalising it seems to make it disappear from my mind. I rely on being clear the first time so that they can enter into the till exactly what I am asking for, as I ask it. I don't expect to have someone questioning me about my order, unless I have ordered something they don't have, or made an order which didn't make sense for some reason. Normally I have to try to get back into the mindset I was in just before I was served, so that I can repeat my order to the person serving.

There are many things which my wife has no problem with that can tip me over the edge. When I travel on a packed train or visit a crowded location, it is like the world has gone into sensory overload, so I withdraw into myself, shutting the world out. My language becomes blunter as I put all my energy into maintaining that inner focus. My hearing starts to shut down, so I find that I can't hear people talking to me. I talk even more nonsense than normal. I find that I have almost no access to real words for things, so I just come out with noises or gestures and looks - or made-up words to try to explain what I mean. And then, despite the fact that I'm the one talking nonsense, I get annoyed when I'm not understood and I feel like I'm having to repeat myself and add emphasis to what I am doing to try to get my point across. Because of my black and white thinking, once I get annoyed, I quickly give up and get stroppy - and unfortunately, it is normally with my wife, as she is the person I'm often with during these times. Once I'm out of the situation, I can calm down very quickly, but in that moment, I think I probably become a very difficult person to be around.

Despite finding 'small things' stressful, I generally find things that others tell me are very stressful, not that stressful. It doesn't mean I don't experience anxiety or anger in those situations, but if I do, they are the correct emotions in my opinion to have at those times, and they are there to be used. So, if I am in a situation where I am being attacked, I will usually be the one with the clear head and reacting with intent, knowing exactly what I am doing and why. I won't be finding the situation stressful in the same way that I find being served in a shop stressful.

One incident, years ago, comes to mind. I was walking along a street with my girlfriend at the time. We were holding a rather mundane, ordinary conversation, when a car driving down the street pulled over, screeching to a halt. The driver jumped out, came over to me, grabbed me, shouting and swearing, and pinned me to the bonnet of his car. I calmly went along with this, let him move me to his car, let him pin me to his bonnet, let him shout and swear at me and say whatever it was he wanted to say. Then, he threw me back towards the pavement, got in his car and drove off. I then picked up the conversation my girlfriend and I were having at the point we had been interrupted. She was breathing oddly, and then stopped me talking to ask about my reaction to the incident. She asked whether I was shaken up by what had happened, as she was still experiencing anxiety. I didn't understand what she was going on about. Why would she be experiencing anxiety?! It was me who was grabbed and shouted at. She said it was a scary incident. I didn't think of it as scary; it was just an incident. I was comfortable with it, and I couldn't understand why she wasn't.

If there is an emergency, generally I'm very good. I prepare for things. So if I stay in a hotel, I check to see how I will get out if the place is burning down and I can't see anything. I watch 'How to survive...' documentaries about surviving plane crashes and other disasters, whereas my wife doesn't like watching these programmes because she sees them as upsetting and scary to watch. I see them as educational - they my save my life one day. They also give me the basis of a structure to follow. It could be that something about a real incident means the exact course of action can't be done, but from what I know, I will quickly come up with a plan B. Then, because there is a plan and a structure, there is nothing to be anxious about. Things may happen while executing that plan, but I feel more comfortable dealing with these things than I do with a shop assistant asking me different questions.

I am very logical about things, which can cause problems. As I have grown up, I have begun to learn that not everything is logical, and that being logical isn't always the right approach to take - just like being honest isn't always the right thing to do. I struggle with both of these. I struggle with not telling the truth, although if I am asked about something where I am about to say I don't like it, and it is something like an idea, I like to see if I can think of something constructive and helpful, rather than just dismissing it. I like to think about what it is I don't like, and what would have to be different for me to like it, so that I have something positive to suggest. With my wife, I will also try not to be in a position where I know I'm going to say something she doesn't want to hear - so that I don't have to lie, because I won't lie, and because I am aware telling the truth sometimes may upset her. I have a tendency to tell the truth accidentally because I haven't avoided the question I was asked in some way, and I haven't been keeping on guard.

For example, my wife was talking to me about something; I thought to myself that I had no interest in what she was talking about, so I started talking about hypnosis, and she pulled me up on this, saying she was telling me something and I just changed the subject. I responded saying I wasn't interested in what she was saying. I had said this before putting my brain in gear and realising what I had said. We continued to talk about what my wife wanted to talk about after this.

I don't make mistakes like this that often now. Part of learning to be in a relationship is learning that everything isn't always about my own interests. I am also gradually learning about when people aren't interested in what I am saying. I find it terribly difficult to recognise when people have got bored or when a conversation should end. It is always stunted and awkward. I just talk until the other person says they have to go, or until I say I have to go. I don't know how else to end a conversation or interaction.

I seem to over-estimate others' interests in subjects I love. When a Milton Erickson documentary was released a couple of years ago, I made sure I ordered it as soon as it became available, because I was worried that so many millions of people would be ordering it that I would miss out, and I had been following the progress of the documentary for years waiting for its release. I didn't want to them have to wait even longer because too many copies were sold by the time I ordered it. I seem to see some things logically, while with other things, any level of common sense seems to go out of the window. Part of what I learn from being in a relationship is having someone who tells me what they think. So, my wife will say, "Milton Erickson isn't that well known and popular, there won't be millions of people buying the documentary" or "you are being repetitive, going on and on about the same thing, you have told me that already". I learn what behaviours and what views of mine are unrealistic.

One thing my wife helps a lot with is challenging my black and white thinking. I spend time as a therapist trying to encourage people to break free from black and white thinking, yet I use it lots myself. If I play computer games, I want them to be a little bit challenging, but I don't want to get stuck at all. Even the slightest moment of getting stuck in a game, and I give up and don't want to play the game any longer. I explain to my wife that I have no interest in the game being challenging; I don't see trying and overcoming the challenge as rewarding. I see having to do the same thing over and over again as tedious. I would rather quit the game, look on the internet and see how it ends; that way, I wouldn't have to play it anymore. There are many areas of my life where I have that attitude, but my wife challenges and pushes me to keep going when I would have quit long ago.

I don't have many friends, and have never had many friends. I personally have never thought about wanting (or, indeed, not wanting) friends, but I am aware that I have moments where I think 'I want to share that with someone' or 'I want to talk to someone'. I am usually happy to talk to pretty much anyone who happens to be there. Sometimes I will want to talk to a specific person - usually because what I want to talk about has most relevance to them, or because I am trying to get something out of it myself and maybe I need that specific person's input or skills. I don't feel a need to always be contacting friends and keeping in touch. I just assume that when I contact them, they will be there. I don't assume they will be annoyed with me for never being in touch, or only being in touch when I want something. I try to be there for anyone who wants my help or support, but only as far as I am comfortable to go; if someone was becoming too needy or taking up too much of my time, I start backing off because I need space, and I quickly feel under pressure and trapped.

When I received my diagnosis, my best friend apologised for not being a good enough friend and for judging me for not calling him often enough. I had never noticed he had been judging me, but I am used to people jumping to conclusions like this, when the simple logical answer is to just talk with the person to find out from them what is going on or what they think.

I was on a training course, when someone came over and started having a go at me saying that I believed I was better than everyone else, and I was arrogant and rude. I asked what made them think that, and they said that, through the whole course, I hadn't interacted with anyone during the break times; I seemed to just sit in a corner all the time, either observing or reading. From this, they had jumped to incorrect conclusions. I explained about myself and they were fine with me. But people will always imprint their view of the world on how they interpret the behaviours of others - as we all do.

I have two friends I see regularly: my best friend I probably see every few months, and we interact perhaps weekly to fortnightly online or via text messages; and another friend I see every month or so - we interact via text message and phone every couple of weeks. The main person I see is my wife. I try to make as much time for her as possible, although she still has to pester me to stop working, or else I find myself still working at 2 or 3am.

I don't really have any kind of social life, but occasionally events crop up through my wife's work which we both go to. Since my days working at Butlin's, I have significantly improved my social skills. This is largely to do with learning hypnosis and so learning to read non-verbal behaviour. I struggle with it if I am in a hectic or high stimulation environment, but generally I can notice when people are being friendly, and when they are hostile. I can now see when people are attracted to others, and so much more. I can also handle situations better now, but I am better at using body language and engaging people when it is one-to-one and in a false setting, like a therapy session or job interview, rather than a real setting like a party. Being a hypnotist, I have had experiences where people challenge me to hypnotise them. Normally, it is someone who has been drinking excessively. They normally have friends with them and they have something to prove. Nowadays, I handle the challenge by saying they are correct, and that I can't hypnotise them. I don't want to get into a competition with the person who has something to prove, so I will let them win straightaway. My main social error I still make is sometimes being too blunt and being honest when I am asked questions. My wife's colleagues may ask me about something - like what I think about the food at the party

- and I won't lie when I answer, but the answer may not be what they want to hear. Or, I may accidentally find myself telling one of my wife's colleagues that they are boring me, or that I have no interest in what they have to say. I try not to do these things because I am there representing my wife, and I don't want to have her tell me she is embarrassed by my behaviour.

I still struggle to remember to engage in reciprocal communication. So when people say hello to me, I struggle to think to say hello back, unless that is all I am doing in that moment - if I am walking along, say, it can be tricky. I also have different views, to my wife at least, over when to say please or thank you. If I am in a shop and the shop assistant asks if I want something and I don't want it, I say "no" in a firm tone of voice to make sure they understand I am saying "no". My wife often picks me up on this, saying I come across as being rude and that I should use a softer tone of voice and say "no, thank you". I don't think I am being rude, though; I am just giving the answer to the question I was asked. Because of my wife's comments, though, I try to say "no" differently; but usually when I'm in that type of situation, I find myself doing the same behaviour regardless of how much I try not to. The same goes if I am blunt with my wife's co-workers at events. I don't mean to come across as rude, but I struggle to say and do the correct behaviours that would stop me appearing rude. Usually, I resort to trying to avoid engaging in any conversations with anyone, unless they are about hypnosis or another subject I am interested in.

When my dad was dying, he initially didn't want my brother and I to see him. He thought it would be too upsetting. I was aware he needed support. He had two friends who were trying to do all they could to help him. He wouldn't let professionals help. After a while, he agreed to us seeing him and I started helping him as best as I could. I was very good at tasks I was given, but not very good at other areas of looking after him. He could be lying on his bed, crying and screaming in agony for hours while I was there, and I wouldn't feel anything. It didn't distress or upset me. I was able to practically help wash him and do chores, but I wasn't able to offer the emotional support he wanted. Dad once said to me while he was in pain on the bed that I wasn't very good at this. I could do tasks, but when I saw him in agony, I just stood there, silently, waiting for my next instruction. This highlighted how far I still have to go with my empathetic and social growth.


## Eating as escapology


Food is an interesting topic, because I hate cooking food, yet I'm quite good at cooking; I hate eating food, yet I eat vast quantities of food. I think I have only ever felt full a handful of times in my life. Normally, I stop when the food is gone.

I am aware foods have different tastes, but not significantly aware. I am more interested in their textures. I eat pretty much anything, because food is essentially just something you are shovelling in to your mouth to give yourself energy, but there are some foods I possibly prefer - as I've mentioned before, these are generally foods with the correct texture or consistency. I like sloppy foods - stew-like foods. I like textures like steak, and I like the feeling of eating foods like raw celery.

I have no problem mixing things. So if my dinner is too hot, I don't mind just adding some water to it to cool it down, or any other drink I happen to have lying around.

I will eat anything at any time of the day. I don't understand when people say they can't eat certain foods at certain times. I also don't understand when people say foods are too rich, or too heavy, or other unusual descriptions. My wife has tried to explain these to me, but I have never grasped what they mean. She has said to me before that she couldn't eat a four litre tub of ice-cream in one sitting because it is too rich. I don't understand this. To me, ice-cream is like a drink, you just eat it and it melts, so it isn't particularly filling. I don't understand how this is a problem. I can understand some very milky things can make me feel a bit sick and bloated. I don't really know why, but it is only if I drink them too quickly. If I go slowly, rather than gulping it back, then milk is fine.

I always explain to people not to cook anything special for me, and not to expect praise for food they cook, because I won't appreciate it. For me, it is about quantity not quality. For years (my wife has gradually knocked this out of me), my idea of when food is 'cooked' was that the food is done when I am bored of cooking it. I didn't care whether the food still looked raw or under-cooked; I just ate it once I was bored of wasting my time cooking. I am always waiting for the day when they invent a pill that you can take, perhaps once per day, so that you never have to endure eating. I think I would miss smells of certain foods, but I can't imagine missing the process of eating food itself.

Something I have been aware of from time to time is that people notice I usually wear the same clothes. When I was going into work I would have the same two or three shirts, which I wore all the time. Even though my job didn't have a uniform, I wanted to have work clothes. I like familiarity, so when I find an item of clothing that is comfortable, I want to wear it all the time. When it wears out, I want to buy exactly the same item as a replacement. When I was doing family support work and walking about 45 miles per week during my work week, I wore hiking trainers. When I started doing that work, I wore normal black smart shoes, as we weren't supposed to wear trainers in work, but after a few months, I tore a tendon in my foot. I walked to A&E to see a doctor, and the doctor was asking me questions about what sports I did to try to find out how I sustained the injury.

I explained I didn't do any sports, but I did walk about 45 miles per week in work. He told me that this was what had injured my foot and that I had to either stop doing the job, or find suitable footwear designed specifically for walking. I chose the latter and found a pair of walking trainers which were black and so didn't look too obvious. I wore the shoes for probably about 4000 miles before they wore away too much to be wearable, so I bought an identical pair. In total, I wore through three pairs of the same trainers during that work. When the final pair was wearing away, I couldn't find the exact same trainers to buy again. This was something that made me think I needed to change jobs. I didn't like the idea of having to take a risk at trying to find a new pair of suitable shoes.

Clothes I wear have to be soft and flowing. Not only do I like to wear soft clothes, but I also feel compelled to touch soft things. Sometimes, I have to put my hands in my pockets to stop myself touching things I shouldn't touch. I have to do the same when I see someone's collar is wrong, or when someone has a hair on their clothes, or some other thing that makes me want to go and neaten it up. I don't like tight-fitting clothes. I like long jackets that flourish, opening and fanning out as I turn around. I often find that my idea of something being soft is different to other people's idea of soft. I can feel things others say are soft, and to me they will feel rough. I don't like wearing clothes I will feel tangled in. If an item of clothing gets too tight or tangled, I can get obsessed and focused on how uncomfortable that area of my body is. I used to wear two types of clothes - either bright, bold colours, like fluorescent green silk shirts, or jet black clothes. My wife has never been a fan of these clothes, so as the years have gone by, I have started to develop a more 'normal' style.

I often wear t-shirts which have something to do with the mind or hypnosis on them. It could be obscure, or something very few would understand. As an example, one of my favourite t-shirts has robotic devices on it, and the words 'automatic movement' on it. Automatic (or in hypnosis speak ideo-motor) movement is something hypnotists elicit to get feedback from clients, and to communicate with the deeper part of someone. It is something that happens all the time in everyday life, but hypnotists are trained to look for these unconscious movements, and what they could be communicating from moment to moment. I can comfortably go months wearing the same limited few items of clothes. I don't get 'bored' of wearing the same thing. To me, I have a style I like in my mind, but then I would find that too much effort to wear daily, so I just wear the clothes I feel comfortable in. This can sometimes mismatch with the weather. My wife used to complain that I always wore the same long leather jacket, all day every day, whether it was the height of summer or the depths of winter.

The good thing about the leather jacket, and one of the key reasons for always wearing it, was that it housed all of my gadgets. At that time there was an explosion of different ideas for music devices, and I also always wanted to be prepared. So I had a belt which had a portable CD player, cassette player, hard drive MP3 player and a minidisc player attached to it. I always carried a small umbrella hooked onto the inside coat pocket, a Swiss army knife in my coat, a small telescope/microscope, and a torch - just in case I needed any of these things.

In my backpack (again, once I found one that was comfortable to carry, I stuck with it and used it until it fell apart), I would have a couple of different books I was reading. Back then I would also have collections of cassette tapes, CDs, minidiscs and spare batteries; and as time went on and I reduced my music devices to just an MP3 player, I have replaced the space with laptops, or tablet PCs, or other portable computer devices, and portable gaming machines, and ebook readers, and notepads to write all my ideas down in, and cameras. My bag is often very heavy because I want everything I could need on me at all times. I would also always have sunglasses on me regardless of the weather, because even on overcast days, I would find the sunlight too bright and it would hurt my eyes.

Struggling with sunlight makes it even more difficult to find my way around, because I am often looking down at the ground. I really struggle to know where I am and to find my way around. I don't really understand why this is, because I am good with maps, and I can work things out once I have a reference point, like a clear landmark that I know. I'm fine when I know where the place I am trying to get to should be in relation to that reference point. But I can be on a bus between Bognor Regis and Chichester, a journey I have made hundreds of times, and I will be staring out of the bus window, confused and trying to find anything familiar that will let me know where I am. Until I work it out, I will be wondering whether I have somehow blacked out and missed Chichester - maybe I am now continuing the journey on to Portsmouth, or maybe I haven't even reached Bognor Regis yet, if I was travelling from a town before Bognor.

I get the same problem walking around towns. Chichester is a simple city to navigate as a shopper: it is a cross of roads, North Street, East Street, South Street, and West Street. I always say you can't really get lost in Chichester, because there are four main roads and a great big Cathedral. Yet, I can be in North Street, for example, and have no idea where I am. I will look around and try to figure it out, and usually, until I see the Cathedral, I will remain confused. I can also never remember where shops are. So if I am in the city with my wife and I go into HMV to look at DVDs, I may come out of there and ask where she is; she will tell me, and I will have no idea where the shop she told me she is in actually is, even though I walk around the city regularly and have done so for years. It isn't even obscure stores I perhaps haven't heard of - it's stores like Boots, or Marks and Spencer's. I even have to try to remember where HMV is when I'm in town and I can't physically see it, yet this is the store in Chichester I probably go into most often.

Another problem I have, which has more of an impact when I am out in public, is talking loudly without realising it. I get really stroppy when it is pointed out to me that I am talking loudly. I don't know why, because all that is happening is that someone is letting me know I am being too loud. But, to me, I believe I am talking quietly almost to the point of whispering. I think that is what annoys me, because it is such a mismatch - to be told I am shouting when I believe I am whispering. Not only do I have a problem with talking loudly without realising, but I also seem to struggle to hear people sometimes. It seems to be intermittent, and I think it is dependent on what distractions there are in the environment that I am trying to block out.

I don't think I have a hearing problem, but I can get really stressed by trying to hear what someone is saying; often, constantly telling the person I can't hear what they are saying can make that person annoyed and stressed with me. Sometimes, even when I hear people, I don't hear their words correctly. I think they have said something that they tell me isn't what they said. Often, I think they have said gibberish, and will repeat back to them in a curious way what I heard them say to try to get an interpretation from them. Sometimes, what I think the person has said doesn't even sound similar to what they actually said. My wife will sometimes laugh at the unusual sentences I think she has said; other times she gets annoyed with having to repeat herself for me to try to understand her.

Something I think is common among people with Asperger's is how we don't like making eye contact. The fact that people are always expecting me to look into their eyes when they're talking to me, and that hypnotists seem to have a reputation for saying look into my eyes, is why I named the book *Look Into My Eyes*. I find what works best for me is looking through people, or past people. Although I will count as I make eye contact - and now, I am more refined than I was as a teenager when I started this habit - I will try to analyse the pattern the other person is using for their eye contact and try to match it. I treat it almost like a dance with the person. Sometimes, I feel too uncomfortable to even make eye contact altogether. This is usually when the person is very interested in what I have to say. Because they are interested in what I am saying, they are usually more attentive and hold eye contact longer, which makes me feel self-conscious if I match this. I instinctively feel that the eye contact I should be giving back should be less than they are giving me, but I can never judge how much eye contact I should be giving, because I can't 'dance' with the other person.

Something that I do now which I hadn't done for years is to read fiction books. I don't read many fiction books, partly because it takes too long - given the choice, I would prefer someone to turn the book into a film, so that I could get through the story quicker. I think I am different to most people I know, in that I just want to know what happens through the story and the conclusion; I don't really get a lot of interest out of all the fluff in the story. So I am happy to read a couple of paragraphs that someone has written describing the whole story from start to finish, rather than perhaps having to read 80,000 words of a novel.

I have heard some people say about enjoying the journey of the story, but I personally don't really care about the journey. I am more interested in having the summarised version that lets me understand what the story was about, and the ending. Apart from reading fiction books I had to read in school, I hadn't read any fiction since being a child. What changed was having an idea for a story in 2000. I thought the idea would make a good film, or book. I was talking to someone about it, and they said that my story sounded a little bit like a Dean Koontz novel called *Lightning*. I didn't want to write a story like something someone else had already written, so I felt I had to read this book. When I saw the size of the novel, I decided I wasn't going to even attempt it.

Some time later, my wife told me that I should start with a short Dean Koontz novel to give me a taste of his writing and perhaps ease me into whether to read *Lightning* or not. She gave me a copy of *Ticktock*, which I read in one sitting, because each chapter ended on a cliff-hanger and I had to complete the pattern, so I read on - but then I had to finish the chapter, so read on. That ended on a cliff-hanger, so I had to read on to complete the chapter, and before I knew it I had completed the book. I decided that, if this is what Dean Koontz books are like, maybe I would manage *Lightning*. I read it, and found that it wasn't like the story I had come up with, so I got on with writing my story - the first long piece of writing I had done. I also decided that I wanted to read other Dean Koontz novels, so I ended up buying and reading every single novel he has written, under his name and under pen names, including his old science-fiction novels and his children's stories. I haven't really tried novels by any other authors, and I doubt I will unless something catches my attention. I have read a few other random novels, because they happened to be about hypnosis or the mind, but Dean Koontz is really the only novelist I have read.

One thing I have a problem with, which can sometimes get out of hand, is picking. If for example, I rub my hand around my face and suddenly feel a single hair that doesn't feel right on my face, I will pick at my face endlessly trying to get the hair. If I am at home, or in a location where I can get some tweezers, then I can use these and the problem is resolved straightaway; but if I don't have access to tweezers or I'm in a location, like on a training course, where it wouldn't be appropriate to just walk out and go to the bathroom to get the hair, I will spend my time picking at it to try to get it. I have picked holes in my face and body before trying to get hairs that are in the wrong place. The same happens around my cuticles, if I find a small bit of skin which is wrong and annoying me. I can pick for hours at a time. Sometimes, I will be in a situation where there is a simple solution (like going and getting tweezers), but instead I start picking and get so engrossed in trying to pick that I don't think of getting tweezers. I can pick needlessly for hours.

**Defining who I have become**

I have had many role models over the years. As a child, I looked up to Superman as someone who embodied how I would want to be as an adult. As I grew up, I also looked up to Spock and *Star Trek The Next Generation*'s Data, as two characters who struggled to understand humans. Both had different perspectives - Spock was comfortable being Spock, whereas Data wanted to try to be as human as possible. I too was comfortable with who I was, but I also wanted to understand others, and I wanted some aspects of myself to be more 'normal'. I also had Sam Beckett from *Quantum Leap* as a role model. He treated people well and wanted what was best for others, often putting others' wellbeing and happiness ahead of his own. When I started reflecting on who I have become as an adult, I started to realise how similar I had become to the role models I had growing up. I continue to like these role models as much now as I always have. I don't understand people 'growing out of' interests, or things they liked when they were younger. I like all the same things I have always liked.

Finding the book *The Magic of Thinking Big* had a huge impact on me. It gave me hope and helped me to understand that I could achieve things in life. The information in this book isn't the sort of information taught in school. In school, the most helpful thing that shaped who I have become was my science teacher giving me advice about writing what I would say to someone if they were asking me questions about what I did - rather than just bluntly writing a one-line answer stating what I had done.

I have been hugely defined by hypnosis. I live and breathe it; there isn't a single day goes by where I don't do hypnosis. I spend most of my time thinking about hypnosis, and it taught me my first skills in understanding non-verbal behaviour and learning how to influence and communicate with others. I have Paul

McKenna to thank for this, and over the years - with thousands of hours of training, practicing, studying - I have learnt so many skills and ways of understanding people. I find I do a lot of this unconsciously, but I still struggle if I am in situations where I'm not as easily able to be choreographing myself. Linked to hypnosis is the influence that Milton H Erickson MD has had on me, and Bruce Lee. Both of them had a similar approach of being flexible and treating everyone as individuals - not being tied to any one system or model. Both had a positive philosophical outlook on life and the world. Milton Erickson also pioneered ways of communicating and helping others that have had far-reaching consequences on many areas of therapy and change work. His work also teaches about having a goal, the importance of close observation and utilising those observations. This way of thinking has shaped how I interact with others; it has turned me from behaving robotically and following clear structures to using flexible structures, and almost 'dancing' with people - being more graceful in what I do.

The biggest influence in my life has been my wife. A clear sign of this was when I gave my speech at our wedding. I wasn't nervous through the wedding, as everything was planned and should have carried out as planned. Some bits that were likely to ruin the plans were getting me frustrated and angry, but it was nothing I wasn't prepared for. The speech, however, definitely didn't go as planned. When it came to me doing my speech, I had practiced it a couple of times just to make sure I was able to do it just glancing at the notes I had written down. I didn't expect any kind of reaction with my speech - my job was to thank everyone for coming, thank the caterers, and thank my wife for marrying me, before telling her how much I love her and saying a bit about how we met. What confused me was that I started crying. I couldn't understand why I started crying because, as my best friend had said, I am like Spock: I don't do 'getting emotional'. The only way I can describe my experience of this is like a computer suddenly crashing. It took me by surprise, as if my brain had just fried.

This is one of the biggest changes my wife has helped me with. When we met in 2001, I was cold - although I tried to meet her needs for hugs and affection. But as the years went on, I started crying at happy and sad films, and now find I cry really easily at these films - yet real things still don't often cause me to cry or get upset. My wife encourages me to socialise - to not be a hermit - although at the same time, she isn't overly social, so we don't go out often. She talks to me about me and teaches me to not just focus on me, but also to focus on her. I believe that, for anyone with Asperger's, being in a healthy relationship can help you make changes to those parts of you that you need to work on, because you put effort into learning to put someone else first, and to see how you can meet their needs. It isn't easy to transfer these skills to the real world, to being the same with others, but you are taking the first step. I definitely feel I probably come across better with others now because of my relationship with my wife.

My wife has given me the strength to believe in myself as a person; she accepts me for who I am and helps me to accept myself. Some aspects of me may be areas I would like to change and wish were different - and they may change, as I continue to develop - but I accept myself for who I am now, and I know I have at least one person on my side. She may get frustrated with aspects of me from time to time, but she accepts me for who I am. I think everyone else in my life also accepts me, but my wife understands me the most, and is willing to do things like make me a den when I need it; she will also pull me up on behaviours I need to stop.

My best friend has also helped me develop. He will challenge me and drag me out to be sociable - and he defined the roles of our relationship as 'Kirk and Spock', which is a very accurate description of us. He also shares in many of my interests, and is curious about learning more and making discoveries. He has also somehow managed to remain a friend for over half of my life, through many life transitions.

I think I am like most others with Asperger's, in that I see it as something that is a part of me, not as something to be cured. It doesn't mean I don't wish I could change some aspects of myself, and I am aware that parents of children with low functioning autism often say they wish there was a cure. As autism is a spectrum, there are some people who have limitations but wouldn't want to be cured of their autism, and others who have significant limitations or debilitating behaviours or traits; they or their carers would like them to be cured.

I have thoughts of concern if there was a pre-birth cure, so that people were no longer born with autism spectrum disorder. My view is that anything which persists in nature is either something that isn't detrimental to the survival of that being, and so it isn't screened out by evolution, or it has advantages to survival. From my studies and my experiences, I feel autism has evolutionary advantages - but to have those advantages, the genes have to be passed on. Some people will be high functioning, and others will be low functioning, but all those who survive will pass on genes linked with a propensity to have 'autism', which - for future generations - could be high or low functioning. Those with high functioning autism, I believe play a role in human progress. It doesn't mean non-autistic people don't advance humanity; it is just that people with high functioning autism are good at focusing on a task and obsessing about it, and so they make discoveries that others wouldn't have made, because they wouldn't have obsessed about that topic in the same way.

Most people who have advanced science have done so through obsessing about a topic and focusing on tasks. They don't seem to get bored of the task or topic and they can keep at it for years. Non-autistic people could obsess and focus on a topic like this, but most people fill their days with many different elements. I can focus on hypnosis for the whole day; I can miss eating and drinking and sleeping for quite some time without being aware of it. I can also comfortably spend each day not interacting with others. Most people want to take breaks; they get bored or tired of what they are doing, and they start talking about it not being stimulating enough. They want to socialise, whether it be having meals with a loved one or with friends, or going to a party. Many people want to progress in a job or role, rather than to do the exact same job for 30 or 40 years. For many with high functioning autism, behaving in this way comes more naturally.

If there was a stone age society and everyone was doing their role - gathering wood or fruits or vegetables, or out hunting - there could be someone with Asperger's who isn't out hunting, is seen as a bit odd and a bit of an outsider, but they have an obsession with how arrows travel through the air, and what makes the arrow go further. This obsession doesn't get anywhere to start with; no-one is really interested. But then, after years of experimenting and learning and trying different things, the Asperger's person suddenly finds a combination of wood for the arrow and a way to shape the flint to make it sharp and streamlined; he perhaps adds the idea of a throwing device, able to propel the arrow. Suddenly, this can give the stone age tribe a survival edge. As society has progressed into the digital age, there are more jobs suited best to those with high functioning autism, which is probably why there is an above average number of people with high functioning autism working within the science and maths professions.

Writing this book has helped me to better understand myself, and has helped me to see both the positive and negative aspects of myself more clearly than I had done previously. I see having Asperger's as giving me strengths many others I meet don't have, but there are also limitations I have which others don't. I sought diagnosis due to discrimination I was experiencing. Prior to seeking diagnosis, I was against getting a label, but when I was being discriminated against, I found that a label may be the best way to get help to stop the discrimination. I have a lot to thank the people in my life for, yet I will probably fail to show them the appreciation they deserve. I feel like I am part-way through a journey of self-discovery. It has only been through looking at who I was, who I am, and who I can be that I can see my place on that journey.

For anyone who thinks they may have Asperger's, I would recommend considering a diagnosis. I wish I had sought a diagnosis a long time ago, rather than waiting for an event like being discriminated against to encourage me to take that step. It can take a long time from approaching a doctor to actually having the assessment; if you are reacting to a problem which is in the here and now, your diagnosis may come too late. I don't know about all doctors, but my GP put me under pressure to justify why I felt he should put an ASD assessment referral through. I found this tough, and I have a lot of experience arguing with professionals to get results, so I would recommend taking a friend in and having things written down - giving behavioural examples that demonstrate meeting the different ASD traits, and including examples from early childhood. You will want a timeframe about when the referral will be sent, when it should arrive with the ASD team, when you should expect to hear from the ASD team, and how long they estimate it will be before you are likely to have the assessment.

Normally, they will say the referral will be sent today, they should have it tomorrow, and the ASD team will be in touch within a couple of weeks. But the assessment appointment may not happen for six to twelve months. Before the assessment, there will be paperwork to fill out - questionnaires about yourself now and in the past - and they will expect someone who knew you well when you were a baby and toddler, ideally the primary carer, to attend the assessment as well. Obviously, this may not always be possible. If it isn't, then they will want to look at another way of proving what you were like when you were very young. If you know this isn't going to be possible, you may wish to think about what other evidence you have, like old school reports from primary school, or medical records.

If you have read this and felt your child may have Asperger's, then the process of what to do to seek a diagnosis is largely similar to what I have just described. You will need to talk to your doctor in the first instance to make a referral. A school may help you and support you, and you may be able to find professional services - like family support services - that can help you. The diagnosis may help to get extra support for your child, both in and out of school.

Many places have parenting support classes and groups specifically for parents of children with autism to look at how best to help your child with possible behavioural problems or difficulties they may have. When you approach the doctor, you need to give clear specific examples of behaviours your child does that make you think they have Asperger's. The doctor needs to write these examples down, or perhaps you can give them an outline of behaviours they can send with the referral. I have known many parents to be disappointed, because the ASD team didn't see their child - they just sent a letter to say to seek alternative support. This is often due to the letter they received not having any information in it which ticks the boxes for ASD. They need to see that the child's problems are in all areas of their life - home, school, and out in the community - and that they have been going on since the child was a baby. They need clear examples of how the child behaves. Persistence is often key, and if you can get the support of other professionals, that helps. If your child has Asperger's, then other professionals will see that too, if they know about Asperger's. They can then send supporting information to the Child and Adolescent Mental Health Team, or whichever team in your location deals with diagnosing ASD.

It can be a long road to diagnosis, but it is often a worthwhile and helpful one when you get there. It can open doors to support, and it can give a focus that explains why the Asperger's person is different. They now have a subject they can study and learn about, as can those who support that person, and they can now identify areas they need to work on and develop, and look at how to develop those areas.

I am probably biased, but I think everyone with Asperger's should learn hypnosis and start hypnotising people. The more people you hypnotise, the more you start to learn about social communication skills and human nuances, and how to adapt to different people. You learn how recognise minimal cues and behaviours of others, and this is one of the most invaluable skills anyone could ever possess.

15724708R00142

Printed in Great Britain
by Amazon